BEYOND THE CHINA MYTH

BEYOND THE CHINA MYTH

Inside — and Against — Keyu Jin's The New China Playbook

MARCO DEUROPA

AD
VERITATEM

Published by Ad Veritatem

ad.veritatem@mail.com

Contents

PART IV

AGAINST JIN, WITH JIN: A CRITICAL PATH

Introduction

This book was born of a paradox. Never has China stood so firmly at the center of the world, and never have we perceived it through an image so blurred, distorted, and torn between fascination and fear. On one side lies the historic success of a model that has lifted hundreds of millions out of poverty; on the other, a political system that concentrates and retains power, controls information and society, and seems afraid even of its own shadow. In between stretches a vast grey zone made of impressive economic dynamics, latent fragilities, rapid transformations, and unresolved contradictions.

Keyu Jin's *The New China Playbook* has the rare merit of explaining China from within, without resorting to the ideological caricatures that dominate Western discourse. Jin presents a rational country, oriented toward development, more complex and less threatening than the newspaper headlines suggest. Yet for that very reason, her analysis is incomplete. To truly speak about China, one must also speak of what cannot be said from within China itself: the political dimension of its historical project, the social cost of its stability, the blind spot of a system that risks suffocating its own innovative energy, and above all the fact that China is not merely an economic model but a form of power.

This book sets out to do what many avoid: not to choose between enthusiasm and alarm, between demonization and apology, but to restore China to its full complexity. To do so, I follow a twofold path. First, I take seriously what Jin affirms—China's strengths, its internal mechanisms, its systemic innovations—and I acknowledge how profoundly the West has misunderstood the real functioning of the Chinese system. Second, I state openly what Jin cannot say—the structural limits of the model, the political contradictions within it, the fragilities of the social contract, the expanding logic of total security, the stagnation of productivity, the geopolitical risks.

China is not an enigma; it is a tension. A country that has succeeded where others have failed, yet now faces challenges that no nation of its size has ever confronted. A country that runs fast, yet risks running into thin air. A country the world observes—often with prejudice, almost always with inadequate conceptual tools.

The aim of this book is to provide those tools. Not to deliver a final judgment—China cannot be assessed through prefabricated moral or ideological categories—but to understand. To understand that its success has real and rational foundations; to understand that its fragilities run deep; to understand that its rise determines not only its own fate but ours as well. And to understand, finally, that China is a mirror: it reflects the limits of Western neoliberalism and the limits of authoritarianism alike. Only by recognizing both truths can we begin to form a more honest reading of the twenty-first century.

PART I

JIN'S NARRATIVE: PROMISES AND AMBIGUITIES

The "New Playbook": What Keyu Jin Is Really Saying

THE CENTRAL THESIS: A THIRD WAY BETWEEN SOCIALISM AND CAPITALISM

The first—and not even particularly veiled—claim of Keyu Jin's book is almost classificatory in nature: China, she argues, is neither socialist nor capitalist. Or rather: it has inherited a socialist institutional structure, adopted with remarkable speed the instruments of global capitalism, and yet coincides with neither model. It is a new, hybrid body that forces the Western observer to suspend the categories through which the twentieth century has been interpreted. Hence the ambition of the title: *The New China Playbook* does not merely aim to describe China; it seeks to rewrite the manual needed to understand it.

The notion of a "third way" may sound like a familiar rhetorical device, one of the many formulas used to describe mixed economies or politically non-aligned systems. But the third way Jin proposes is something different. It is not a compromise, nor a midpoint between two extremes, nor an intermediate square on the ideological chessboard. It is instead the claim that China has created a development model in which state and market are not located at opposite ends of a balance, but are intertwined to the point of becoming indistinguishable. The categories "socialist" and "capitalist," Jin argues, are far too impoverished to capture this dynamic fusion. They do not describe what China has become: a system in which planning does not replace the market, and the market does not constrain planning, but each reinforces the other in ways that challenge the theoretical assumptions of Western economics.

To support this thesis, Jin begins with a point that surprises many Western readers: China, she says, is in some respects one of the most authentically "capitalist" societies in the world. Not institutionally—there is no separation of powers, no entrepreneurial freedom in the liberal sense, no independent legal protection of property rights. And yet, if one looks at the actual behaviour of economic actors—the entrepreneurial dynamism, the ferocity of local competition, the levels of private investment, and the degree of social mobility linked to economic success—China appears as a laboratory of extreme capitalism. At the same time, Jin observes, the country remains deeply marked by a socialist imaginary: a widespread sense of community and social duty, expectations of public protection, trust in the state as a collective organiser. The result is a hybrid that imitates no pre-existing model.

According to Jin, this hybrid rests on three pillars. The first is the state—but not the oppressive, paralysing state of Western clichés. Jin speaks of "state capacity": the ability to mobilise resources, coordinate economic actors, and channel credit and investment toward strategic aims. In her reading, the Chinese state is not an obstacle to growth but the invisible conductor creating the conditions for the market to operate at maximum intensity.

The second pillar is what she calls "local competition": a system in which mayors, governors, and party officials compete fiercely to attract firms, experiment with policies, and produce measurable results. The usual Western image of China as a rigid, vertically organised pyramid thus appears misleading: the country is also a dispersed laboratory, a mosaic of local experiments in economic policy where success is rewarded and imitated.

The third pillar is private entrepreneurship, which Jin describes as surprisingly dynamic, innovative, and risk-oriented. In her telling, China did not grow merely through public investment or cheap labour, but through millions of entrepreneurs navigating a brutally competitive environment with extraordinary speed.

From this triad—capable state, local competition, aggressive entrepreneurs—emerges the "model" Jin sets against Western simplifications. The structure of her book follows the three canonical actors of the economy: consumers, firms, and the state. But the conclusion is always the same: none of the three behaves in China as Western experience would lead us to expect. Consumers are not as crushed as commonly assumed; firms are not suffocated by state control; the state is not the antithesis of the market. It is a deliberately counterintuitive picture, built to dismantle what the West considers "obvious."

In this sense, the book is less descriptive than it appears. It is a polemical text, an intellectual rejoinder aimed above all at the West. Jin seeks to demolish what she calls "Western mythology": the idea that economic development necessarily requires liberal institutions; that an economy led by a single party is destined to fail; or that China's success is built on statistical deception, useless infrastructure, and repression. Against such myths, Jin offers a coherent narrative of how China modernised its system without adopting Western norms—and how this process was not only possible, but effective.

Her most implicit thesis—and this is where the book becomes political, though it never states it openly—is that the Western model is no longer universal. China, in her view, is not a temporary anomaly, living through an exceptional parenthesis destined to end in a return to "normality." Rather, it is an alternative form of modernity: one that combines political authoritarianism, competitive capitalism, strategic centralisation, and operational decentralisation. A form that—according to Jin—can endure, adapt, and even teach lessons to the West.

For the present writer, all this is a point of departure, not a point of arrival. Taking Jin's thesis seriously means doing what the West often fails to do: listening before criticising, suspending categories before applying them. But taking it seriously does not mean accepting it. The questions that will guide the entire book are twofold: Is China really what Jin describes? And even if it were, what is the human, political, and psychological cost of such a model?

For now, we have reconstructed Jin's argument faithfully. In the chapters that follow, we will begin measuring the distance between the promise of the "playbook" and the reality of contemporary China.

STRATEGIST STATE, DISCIPLINED MARKET, ELITE-LED GROWTH

The decisive hinge of Jin's "new playbook" is the image of an economic system in which the state does not limit the market but structures it, and in which the market does not correct the state but becomes its operational extension. In her account, this symbiosis takes the shape of a very precise triangle: strategist state, disciplined market, elite-led growth. Seen through Western eyes, such a triangle almost sounds like a contradiction in terms; yet in Jin's vocabulary, it is the key to understanding twenty-first-century China.

The strategist state is, first of all, a state that claims the right not only to define the conditions of growth, but its direction. It does not merely create a favourable environment for investment: it decides which investments are to be encouraged, which sectors must become drivers of development, which technologies are to be protected and which accelerated. In her telling, this power is not arbitrary, not the vertical imposition of a blind authority: it is the expression of a technical and administrative capacity that, in her view, the West has lost. For Jin, the Chinese state possesses a kind of collective intelligence made of five-year plans, macroeconomic analysis integrated into political decision-making, a local bureaucracy that experiments and adjusts, and a system of rewards and sanctions that incentivises results rather than loyalty. It is, so to speak, a technical elite that "administers" the future.

This strategic intervention is paired with a very specific conception of the market: a disciplined market, free to compete, innovate, and take risks, as long as it does so within a framework of stability defined by the state. It is not an anarchic market, nor a market in which private initiative can jeopardise the overall order of the system. It is a market born of the awareness that private-sector efficiency does not substitute for public-sector vision. The image Jin suggests is almost choreographic: the market dances, but the score is written elsewhere. Private enterprise is free, but not sovereign. Competition is fierce, but not subversive. Start-ups may grow explosively, but they must learn to live with the constraints imposed by a political power that reserves the right to intervene—sometimes abruptly—whenever it perceives systemic risks. For Jin, this combination of operational freedom and strategic discipline allows Chinese capitalism to be more dynamic, more flexible, more agile than its Western counterpart.

The third vertex of the triangle is the most delicate of her claims: Chinese growth, she argues, is led by elites. Not in the banal sense of a rich, privileged class, but in the technical sense of a selected, competent elite trained to interpret data, channel resources, and make rapid, bold decisions. Jin contends that the Chinese bureaucracy—at least at the middle and upper levels—is neither a feudal court nor an apparatus paralysed by ideology, but a functional meritocracy: a corps of administrators competing on the basis of measurable results rather than personal connections. Growth would thus not be the product of chance, nor of a spontaneous impulse of the market, but of the convergence between the "enlightened" choices of this elite and the dynamic response of entrepreneurs.

This image—strategist state, disciplined market, competent elite—is not purely descriptive. It contains an implicit judgement: China has achieved what the West no longer manages to do. The Western state appears as weak, slow, captured by lobbies and electoral constraints; the Western market as distracted, financialised, unable to steer real growth; Western elites as fractured, trapped in ideologies that paralyse action. China, by contrast, appears as a large coordinated organism, a machine in which every organ knows its function and performs it without obstructing the others.

The allure of this narrative is obvious: it suggests the existence of a system that does not sacrifice economic freedom on the altar of authority, nor stability on the altar of the market. A system that, at the limit, seems to overcome the structural flaws of the United States and Europe: fragmented decision-making, dependence on hypertrophied financial markets, and the inability to plan long-term investment. China appears as what the West secretly longs for: a place where someone is still able to decide—and to decide well.

And yet it is precisely here that a fracture opens. Is the image of the strategist state real, or is it a selective myth? Is the market truly disciplined, or is it constantly threatened by political unpredictability? And above all: is this growth-guiding elite truly a meritocracy, or is it an opaque structure in which corruption, internal struggles, purges, and political loyalty count more than talent? Jin presents a harmonious triangle; reality may be more unstable, more contradictory, more ambiguous. Before tackling these questions—which go to the heart of the Chinese model and its future—we must fully grasp the internal coherence of the story Jin tells. It is an elegant, seductive narrative, capable of ordering complex phenomena with a simplicity that attracts. But for any model to be credible, it must withstand the test of facts. That will be our next test.

JIN'S STRONGEST AND MOST INNOVATIVE ARGUMENTS

Jin's strongest arguments do not lie in her political conclusions, but in her ability to grasp certain essential features of the Chinese experience that Western analysis has often ignored or only half understood. This is where her book becomes genuinely useful: not when it proposes a general theory of the Chinese model, but when it sheds light on concrete passages of the country's development that tend to escape ideological readings. And this is perhaps why Jin provokes both enthusiasm and irritation:

she forces readers to rethink many of the automatisms through which we interpret China.

The first truly solid argument concerns state capacity. Jin insists that throughout China's modernisation, the state has not simply been a controller but above all an enabler. And she is right: the West, accustomed to identifying the state with slowness and bureaucracy, struggles to recognise the administrative elasticity China has developed since the 1980s. Experimental decentralisation—the logic by which different provinces test different policies, with the possibility of generalising what works—has genuinely been a driver of institutional innovation. This is not propaganda: data, administrative histories, and local reforms all confirm this dynamic. Jin reminds Western readers that a one-party system does not necessarily equal a rigid machine; it can be, at certain stages, a widespread laboratory of economic policy. This is a point that deserves acknowledgment.

A second convincing element is the fierce competition among firms, regions, and local administrations. Here Jin captures an essential feature of Chinese capitalism: competition is no less intense than in the West—indeed, often it is far more so. Nothing comparable exists in the Western world to the level of pressure local governments place on themselves to demonstrate tangible economic results: local GDP growth, increased investment, creation of industrial parks, construction of infrastructure capable of attracting businesses. This dynamic produces distortions, of course (which Jin tends to downplay), but it also generates administrative innovation and speed of execution. When Jin observes that many Chinese cities function like territorial start-ups run by administrative elites playing high-risk games, she is not stretching reality; she is describing a distinctive aspect of China's modernisation.

A third solid aspect is the centrality of private entrepreneurship. The West has often reduced China to a country of state-owned enterprises kept alive by the Party. Jin reminds us that the true explosion of growth was driven by millions of small and medium-sized private firms, by an entrepreneurial fabric that has moved with surprising speed and determination. Much of China's technological innovation—from digital technologies to robotics, from logistics to services—was born in this competitive environment, not within the state apparatus. Many analysts acknowledge this point, and Jin highlights it with clarity: anyone who wants to understand contemporary China cannot ignore its aggressive, growth-oriented private capitalism.

Jin is particularly persuasive when she discusses the asymmetry of perceptions between China and the West. Her argument here is simple but important: Westerners judge China using categories that belong to their own historical experience, not to China's. They see only authoritarianism, not coordination capacity; they see only the absence of formal rights, not the scale of economic and social mobilisation; they see only the risks of political control, not the stability it has long guaranteed. This is not a defence of the regime, but a reminder that Chinese modernisation has unfolded through a different political language, and that it makes little sense to interpret it with the wrong conceptual lenses. In this respect, Jin offers a genuinely useful correction: she invites readers to suspend automatic judgments and observe China as a historically specific object.

A fifth innovative element concerns domestic demand, which Jin describes with an attention many Western analysts have lacked. The image of China as an "export giant" is only partially accurate: in recent years, the growth of urban consumption, the emergence of a digital middle class, and the role of platforms have reshaped the structure of demand. Jin shows, with considerable effectiveness, how China is becoming an economy in which urban consumers—more educated, more mobile, more demanding—carry increasing weight. Again, her contribution is not revolutionary, but it is important: it reminds us that China is not frozen in its past, and that the transformation of consumption is a structural phenomenon.

Finally, Jin introduces an argument that is seldom explored in the West: social cohesion. Again, this does not mean endorsing her conclusions, but acknowledging that she touches a real point. The ability of Chinese society to accept collective sacrifice, to endure extreme work rhythms, to mobilise around shared goals, is not a propagandistic invention. It is a historical, cultural, psychological fact. Jin interprets this cohesion as a competitive advantage: a country that does not fracture easily, that does not paralyse itself over every political crisis, that accepts central directives with relative docility. It is an optimistic reading—perhaps too optimistic—but it captures something the West struggles to grasp: China is not only an authoritarian regime; it is a society with a strong social code of obedience and collective responsibility.

These are the points at which Jin is most convincing: when she describes, when she observes with nuance, when she corrects Western simplifications, when she reveals what the West fails to see. This is where her book becomes genuinely useful: in recognising the complexity of China's modernisation, in acknowledging what is true, effective, and intelligent in the country's economic trajectory. And it is from here, from this solid foundation, that we will be able to measure its shadows—for the very elements Jin celebrates—the strategist state, social cohesion, local competition, and market discipline—can also become deep vulnerabilities if read attentively and without indulgence. We continue from this point.

HER FUNDAMENTAL BLIND SPOT: POLITICS IS NOT BACKGROUND NOISE

The clearest impression one gets from reading Jin is that politics is always present but relegated to the background, like a noise that interferes with the melody rather than shaping it. Her entire narrative works only insofar as the Communist Party is treated as an almost neutral entity, a kind of stable frame within which the economy unfolds with great creativity. But this abstraction is the decisive blind spot: in China, politics is not the frame of the economy—it is its fabric. It is not a lower level of analysis, but an active principle that penetrates every decision, every firm, every local administration. And it is precisely this that distinguishes China from any other model of "disciplined capitalism."

Jin speaks often of state capacity, administrative competence, and technical elites pursuing long-term goals. But these elites do not exist independently of the political mechanism that selects them, rewards them, punishes them, and purges them. Even the very notion of an administrative meritocracy loses much of its explanatory power once one acknowledges that the careers of Party cadres depend as much on political loyalty as on economic performance, and that internal Party dynamics are neither transparent nor linear. What Jin describes as technical rationality can, from one day to the next, become the instrument of a purge, a power rebalancing, or a sudden political priority. Nothing is further from a stable institutional laboratory than a bureaucracy exposed to the political cycles of an authoritarian regime.

The very image of the strategist state, in its idealised form, requires the state to be a coherent entity, endowed with continuity and capable of learning from its errors. But the Party is not a neutral institution: it is a political organism with its own internal struggles, ideological shifts, periods of opening and of closure, phases of liberalisation and of repression. The state's intervention in the economy is guided not only by technical criteria, but by changing political priorities. One need only recall that entire economic sectors have been abruptly hit by political campaigns—private education, platform technology, real estate—without consultation or transition periods. One night, an algorithm complies with the rules; the next night, it is illegal. In such an environment, the market is disciplined, yes—but disciplined by something whose form can shift unpredictably.

Even the account of local competition—the race among provinces and cities—loses its descriptive force if one forgets that these administrations do not answer to citizens-voters but to the Party. The competition is not driven by political pluralism or by democratic accountability, but by a hierarchical mechanism that may prioritise growth at certain moments and political stability or "ideological purity" at others. The same mayors Jin portrays as competitive managers are also officials who must interpret ambiguous political signals, and who risk their careers —or worse—if they misread the direction of the wind.

But the most problematic aspect of Jin's narrative concerns her portrayal of Chinese society as a coherent body, willing to accept collective sacrifices for shared goals. Up to a point, this description captures something real. But it overlooks the fact that this cohesion is sustained by a political control system with no equivalent in advanced economies: digital surveillance, preventive censorship, selective repression of dissent, and algorithmic governance of civic life. None of this is background noise—it is the mechanism that allows the model to function. Jin separates the economy from politics to show that the Chinese model is efficient; but such a separation is impossible in reality. The desire for social stability, which she interprets as a cultural trait, is also the product of a political system that drastically limits the space for conflict and uncertainty.

Ultimately, her blind spot lies in excluding the possibility that politics—in the full sense of the word—might be a source of structural vulnerability rather than merely a source of stability. Authoritarianism appears as an acceptable cost, at times even as an organisational advantage, but never as an endogenous risk to the system. And yet this is precisely the knot the rest of this book must confront: not China as a sum of local administrations, dynamic firms, and emerging consumers, but China as a political regime that decides who rises and who falls, that steers the economy as much as it interprets it, that uses growth as a tool of legitimacy and, at the same time, as a possible source of instability. Politics is not the backdrop against which the economic story is projected: it is the very substance of the model. And it is in the relationship between economic effectiveness and political control, between innovation and authority, between growth and fear, that the future of China must be read—far beyond the playbook Jin offers us.

Does Chinese Meritocracy Really Exist?

LOCAL GOVERNANCE, CADRE SELECTION, INCENTIVES, AND CAREERS

When Jin speaks of China's alleged meritocracy, her point of departure is always the same: the local level. That, she suggests, is where the true nature of the system reveals itself—not in Party ceremonies in Beijing, not in five-year congresses, but in municipalities, prefectures, and provincial administrations where thousands of cadres stake their careers on concrete outcomes. Her thesis, stated simply, is this: Chinese governance is performance-based. Advancement does not come through seniority, nor solely through political loyalty, but through the proven ability to grow the economy, attract investment, and improve social indicators. The country, in her view, is governed by a class of officials who resemble managers more than bureaucrats.

To support this thesis, Jin invokes a real feature of the system: for decades, the careers of local officials have been formally tied to a set of indicators. For a long time, the most important was the growth rate of GDP in the territory they administered; later, at least on paper, other factors were added—employment, investment, fiscal revenues, and occasionally even environmental or social criteria. In theory the logic is clear: every city, county, and province functions as a kind of competitive laboratory; those who govern their territories effectively earn promotion, those who fail are transferred or removed. This is the so-called "tournament promotion" model: a permanent contest in which advancement is the reward for outperforming one's peers. In this sense, the idea of meritocracy is not without foundation. If one looks at the résumés of many Chinese leaders, one often finds a long sequence of local postings, each leaving behind industrial zones, infrastructure, urban plans, or policies designed to attract private enterprise. This is not mere rhetoric: in many cases, the ascent to senior Party positions has indeed passed through concrete experiments in governance.

But the way Jin presents this mechanism is selective from the outset. In her reconstruction, the relationship between performance and promotion is linear: the official who "delivers" rises, the one who fails falls. In practice, the reality is far more ambiguous. First, because the indicators that matter are not always the same, nor are they always transparent. For many years, what made a local cadre a "good administrator" was almost exclusively GDP growth—no matter the cost. Building roads, bridges, empty residential districts, or half-occupied industrial parks inflated economic aggregates and appeared, on paper, as proof of dynamism. Careers were built on this logic: generating numbers rather than solving structural problems. Meritocracy here takes on a paradoxical form: it does not reward substantive merit—sustainably improving life in a territory—but statistical merit, the ability to boost whichever indicators the centre wishes to see rise.

Then there is the issue of hidden incentives. If my career depends on short-term GDP growth, I have every incentive to take decisions that produce visible effects quickly, even if they create long-term fragilities. This is precisely what happened with the explosion of local government debt, with financing vehicles accumulating enormous liabilities to fund development projects of uncertain value. For years, these mechanisms were tolerated—indeed encouraged—because they made it possible to display impressive performance. The meritocracy of local cadres thus entered a vicious cycle: the official who pressed hardest on the accelerator was rewarded, until the debt became unsustainable; and once the music changed, it emerged that many "successful" careers rested on fragile foundations. Jin tends to overlook this contradiction: she accepts the official narrative of "merit-based selection" without fully questioning the quality of the merit being rewarded.

Even at the level of cadre selection, her narrative indulges in a degree of idealisation. It is true that the Party has developed more elaborate evaluation procedures: rotations between posts, mandatory experience in poorer or more challenging regions, periodic assessments, continuous training. But all of this occurs within a system where political loyalty is not an accessory criterion but a permanent condition of survival. An economically brilliant but politically misaligned official is, at best, vulnerable; at worst, doomed. The meritocracy Jin describes is thus interwoven with a logic of political control that she does not analyse. It is not enough to say that "performance matters"—one must ask *which* performance, judged by *whom*, with what margin for criticism, and with what possibility of dissenting from central directives without being punished.

The dynamics of incentives and careers—which Jin presents as the product of a collective rationality—are in fact shaped by shifting political phases. In periods of greater openness, administrative elites were encouraged to experiment, to seek new approaches, to collaborate with private entrepreneurs. In periods of tightening, the same competitive mechanisms have been reabsorbed into a more centralised logic, where the priority is no longer simply growth but the prevention of any form of instability. This means that incentives can shift abruptly: what was yesterday rewarded—taking risks, expanding local debt, embracing growth at any cost—can suddenly become evidence of irresponsibility or deviation from new directives. The official whom Jin portrays as a rational manager is, in reality, an actor navigating a double uncertainty: economic and political.

And yet, compared to many Western caricatures, Jin does capture something real: the Chinese system is not a monolith in which every decision descends from above to be executed passively. There truly is an intermediate level—what we would call local governance—where intense games of power, ambition, and administrative creativity take place. Many policies we now consider "national" were first born in a remote province, a second-tier city, or an industrial district built in a few years. Many leaders have indeed built their careers on concrete achievements. But reducing all this to a linear meritocracy means forgetting that the stakes are not only growth, but conformity to a political system that decides unilaterally who is "meritorious" and who no longer is. If local governance is a laboratory, it is a laboratory under perpetual supervision, where administrative science can at any moment be interrupted by an act of political will.

If Chinese meritocracy exists at all, it is not a natural feature of the system but an unstable equilibrium between competence and obedience, between results and loyalty, between economic indicators and political signals. It is precisely in this tension that it must be examined—if one refuses to settle for the domesticated version Jin offers.

THE IMAGE OF CHINA AS AN "EFFICIENT STATE": MYTH, REALITY, PROPAGANDA

The idea of China as an efficient state is perhaps the most powerful—and at the same time the most ambiguous—core of Jin's narrative. It is powerful because it touches one of the West's deepest wounds: its inability to decide, to plan, to build infrastructure, to maintain a vision beyond the electoral cycle. It is ambiguous because it conflates three different dimensions—administrative reality, foundational myth, and political propaganda—treating them as if they were one and the same. In Jin's account, the Chinese state is the exact opposite of the paralysed Leviathan that dominates advanced democracies: it is agile, experimental, capable of rapid learning, endowed with a competent bureaucracy and a leadership that knows how to set objectives and pursue them with discipline. And yet this image, while containing elements that are undeniably true, is also the product of careful selection: it highlights the successes and silences the cracks, presents the exception as the rule, and transforms propaganda into a kind of sociological truth.

That the Chinese state has acted with remarkable speed and determination during various phases of its modernisation is indisputable. Infrastructure built in a matter of years, urban transformation on a massive scale, the expansion of high-speed rail, the electrification of the country, the management of strategic sectors such as energy and telecommunications—all of this testifies to an executive capacity that many Western governments can only lament. Experimental decentralisation has genuinely produced administrative innovations; the ability to mobilise human and material resources at short notice is equally real; and the presence of technically trained cadres is no legend. It is therefore entirely reasonable to speak of a capable state, and many scholars have done so for years. But to speak of administrative capacity is one thing; to speak of efficiency as a structural, almost ontological, feature of the Chinese political system is quite another. It is here that the gap between reality and myth begins.

The myth of efficiency arises from the fact that China enjoyed, for decades, a historical advantage: a poor country can grow very quickly by following relatively well-known paths, imitating what has worked elsewhere. Building roads, ports, power plants, and factories is "easy" when one starts from zero and can rely on abundant labour, low wages, and a political system unencumbered by procedural constraints. The speed of China's early modernisation is not proof of intrinsic efficiency, but the manifestation of a favourable historical condition. When the country began confronting complex problems—an ageing population, debt, low productivity, advanced innovation—efficiency faltered. And here the myth begins to dissolve: a state that excels at building physical infrastructure does not necessarily excel at managing a mature, highly interdependent economy.

Then there is the propagandistic dimension, which Jin does not deconstruct—indeed, she implicitly reinforces it. Official rhetoric about state capacity is one of the principal tools through which the Party legitimises its rule. Efficiency, even more than prosperity, forms the basis of its claim to superiority over democracies. The narrative of "Chinese speed" is a political product, carefully constructed through selected examples, highlighted successes, silenced failures, and statistical revisions that make discontinuous processes appear linear. The grand projects that are celebrated are only part of the story; unfinished works, planning errors, environmental costs, ghost cities, and unused infrastructure are also part of the picture. But Jin barely mentions these, as though they were marginal—whereas in fact they form the reverse side of the model.

The image of the efficient state is thus a composite: part reality, part myth, part propaganda. Reality lies in the administrative capacity accumulated in the 1980s and 1990s, in the technical competence of many cadres, in the existence of rapid learning processes. Myth lies in the idea that this capacity is uniform, stable, structural—when in fact it is uneven, historically contingent, and often the result of the energy of particular regions or individuals rather than a coherent national design. Propaganda lies in the political use of this image to justify a system that admits no alternatives: if the state is so efficient, then questioning it appears pointless; if it can accomplish in five years what takes others twenty, then every sacrifice is justified.

What Jin does not say is perhaps the decisive point: an authoritarian state appears efficient only as long as it does not face problems that require transparency, informational pluralism, or unfiltered feedback. Chinese efficiency is real wherever decisions are simple, vertical, and replicable; it becomes opaque—and often ineffective—when complexity requires listening, revising, accepting conflict, tolerating error. Jin's silence on this question—the relationship between efficiency and power—suggests that her image of the state is built more on aspiration than analysis. It is not a matter of denying that China possesses notable administrative capacities; it is a matter of recognising that these capacities are no guarantee of future effectiveness, and that the political price of apparent efficiency may be far higher than her account allows one to imagine.

CORRUPTION, OPACITY, INTERNAL STRUGGLES: THE PART JIN DOES NOT SEE (OR DOES NOT WANT TO SEE)

Jin's narrative about the competence of China's administrative class holds together as long as one looks at the system from the vantage point of economic performance and organisational discipline. But shift the gaze by only a few degrees, and what remains consistently in the shadows in her book becomes visible: structural corruption, opacity in decision-making, and internal Party struggles as constant features of Chinese political life. These are not marginal or pathological elements; they are constitutive dimensions of the system. They are not deviations from the rule, but the rule itself—or at least one of its vital arteries. To ignore them, as Jin does, is to offer a description that is formally coherent yet substantively amputated, unable to capture how the Chinese state actually functions.

Corruption is not a peripheral flaw of the model; historically, it has been its release valve, its most common form of negotiation between centre and periphery, between politics and the economy. For decades, the enormous operational freedom granted to local governments in managing land, contracts, and licences was accompanied by extreme permeability to private interests and clientelism. Administrative careers were often built through personal networks, favours, mutual protection; entrepreneurial fortunes were at times born less from merit or innovation than from political connections. This does not erase the virtuous cases, but it prevents us from presenting meritocracy as the backbone of the system. Jin mentions the problem only in passing, and when she does, she frames it as a historical residue on the verge of disappearing. Reality is more stubborn: corruption has been one of the mechanisms through which the Party has maintained cohesion—tolerating it in some phases to spur growth, repressing it in others to reassert political control. It is a systemic variable, not a disturbance.

Overlaying corruption is a second layer: opacity. The Chinese political system does not allow us to see how decisions are actually made; it does not reveal which forces within the Party matter, which factions prevail, which compromises are struck. The image of a rational, self-correcting state would require transparency; but transparency is incompatible with the nature of the Party. Thus the rationality Jin attributes to the state is always, in the end, an act of faith. What can be observed from the outside is the outcome, not the process. A given decision may stem from technical analysis, from an internal battle, from a sudden order, from the need to produce a scapegoat to restore discipline. To present every outcome as evidence of superior rationality is, in effect, to adopt the perspective the regime wishes to impose.

Internal struggles constitute the third omitted element. Jin speaks of the Party as if it were a unified organism, a kind of vast collective intelligence that learns, coordinates, and corrects. But no serious observer ignores that the Party is traversed by radical competitions for power: between generations, between factions, between geographic blocs, between competing visions of openness and control. Promotions are not merely the result of administrative performance; they are often the product of balances between power groups, of loyalty to dominant figures, of strategic positioning within a political landscape that shifts in waves. The idea that cadre selection is a transparent, results-based contest is naïve; the idea that the state operates as a coherent machine is even more so. Central authorities intervene periodically to rebalance the system, dismantling local power networks, purging leaders who have accumulated too much influence or who embody alternative political visions. Jin does not address any of this, as if it had no bearing on the state's capacity to act coherently.

In reality, the presence of widespread corruption, systemic opacity, and internal struggles is not background noise: it is part of what China *is*. It explains the intermittent nature of administrative efficiency—periods of great momentum alternating with phases of paralysis; bursts of initiative followed by cycles of repression; sudden decisions that overturn months of planning. It is what renders the state's behaviour unpredictable for firms, local officials, and citizens alike. It is what transforms every success of the model into an inherently fragile promise—one that may be confirmed or abruptly reversed depending on internal dynamics that no one can see. Behind the façade of rational governance stands a political system that Jin, consciously or not, chooses to treat as irrelevant. Yet it is precisely this system, with its shadow zones, that determines the limits of any optimistic reading of the Chinese model. To ignore it is not a technical oversight; it is an ideological choice.

The Economic Miracle Explained from Within

URBANISATION, EDUCATION, SAVING: THE REAL INGREDIENTS

When one attempts to explain China's economic growth over the past forty years, one risks oscillating between two extremes: on one side, a miracle narrative attributing everything to the wisdom of the state and the foresight of the Party; on the other, a cynical reading that reduces China's success to nothing more than labour exploitation and a fortunate alignment of favourable conditions. Jin proposes a third path: to show from within what the concrete ingredients of the economic takeoff really were. And in this exercise—despite all the omissions I will later analyse—she touches on several real and often overlooked points. If we want to understand China, we must begin with three structural phenomena that transformed society more rapidly than any government plan: urbanisation, educational expansion, and an extraordinary accumulation of savings. These three factors—more than industrial policy or grand strategic visions—form the backbone of the "miracle."

The first engine is urbanisation. In less than half a century, hundreds of millions of people moved from a rural economy to an urban one, in a process without precedent in human history. Industrial-era Europe took two centuries to make the same journey; China did it in two generations. This population shift was not merely geographical: it was a radical change in productivity. A person who leaves a farming village and finds employment in urban industry or services immediately increases their economic contribution. It is a built-in demographic leap in efficiency. Chinese cities have acted as enormous centrifuges: drawing in young labour, concentrating human capital, and creating agglomeration economies that multiply productivity. No public policy—however efficient—can substitute for the simple fact of relocating hundreds of millions of people from low-productivity to high-productivity sectors. Jin emphasises this, and it is one of her clearest insights: the Chinese miracle begins with population flows, not central visions.

The second ingredient is education. Here China has been more determined than often acknowledged. The expansion of secondary and tertiary education in the 1990s and 2000s produced a vast cohort of young people with increasingly sophisticated technical skills. They were—and are—not intellectual elites comparable to those of the great Western centres, but they constitute an educated, disciplined workforce with a strong scientific orientation. The Chinese education system, with all its limits, has generated millions of engineers, technicians, programmers—the people capable of fuelling first the industrial machine, then the technological one. It is a form of human capital accumulated quietly, without the fanfare of elite universities, but with a demographic power no Western country can match. Jin is right to insist: Chinese innovation did not appear from nowhere; it is not improvisation, but the product of an urbanised, educated generation that found in China's new capitalism a natural outlet.

The third ingredient is saving. In this respect, China is a global statistical anomaly: a savings rate exceeding 40 percent of national income for long stretches of time—almost inconceivable in advanced economies. The reasons are multiple—family-based welfare, lack of safety nets, a culture of sacrifice, political uncertainty—but the effect is one: an immense supply of capital available for investment. The West envies China's ability to finance infrastructure, industry, and research, but rarely asks where the resources come from. They come from a people who saved in almost ascetic fashion for decades. Jin sees in this a competitive advantage: a country able to invest massively without depending on global financial markets can shape its future without being constrained by international volatility. This too is true, at least in part. High savings gave the Chinese government a margin of manoeuvre no democracy could ever obtain, and sustained a growth model based on continuous—and often redundant—investment.

Urbanisation, education, saving: three engines that, when combined, can transform any country, regardless of regime type. There is nothing inherently "Chinese" about these phenomena; they are the same mechanisms that have powered every major development process, from Victorian England to postwar America to Japan's reconstruction. What is "Chinese" is not the process itself, but the scale and speed at which it occurred. Jin is right to insist: the economic miracle cannot be understood by looking only at the political surface; it becomes clear when one examines the subtle movements of population, human capital, and savings. And for this part of her analysis, her voice is genuinely persuasive: she describes structural forces that lie beyond the noise of geopolitics.

The problem—and it will be the core of the next sections—is that Jin tends to interpret these phenomena as evidence of the superiority of the Chinese political model, when in fact they are factors that could operate under any form of government, and that in China have often required an extremely high human cost. Urbanisation was propelled by a household registration system (hukou) that created first-class and second-class citizens; education produced technical excellence but also conformity and immense psychological pressure; high saving was possible only because an adequate welfare system did not exist. The true ingredients of the miracle are real, but they are not a celebration of the model: they are the ground on which the model built its legitimacy—and at the same time the limits it may soon confront. We continue from here.

THE BLOCK ECONOMY: STATE FIRMS, PRIVATE CHAMPIONS, AND THE LOGIC OF POLITICAL ALIGNMENT

To understand the real structure of the Chinese economy, one must abandon the overly simple image of a "hybrid" capitalism in which state and private sectors coexist harmoniously. China is not a laboratory where two separate worlds—public and private—operate each according to its own rationality. Rather, it is a system organised into functional blocs, where the distinction between state-owned and privately owned enterprises matters far less than the position a firm occupies relative to political power. The first question is not: *"Is this firm private or state-owned?"* but: *"Is this firm aligned with the political line of the moment?"* Seen from this angle, the behaviour of economic actors becomes intelligible.

State-owned enterprises (SOEs) are the visible infrastructure of economic power. They control energy, finance, telecommunications, transport, major infrastructure. They are not merely corporations but extensions of state authority: their purpose is to guarantee energy security, price stability, employment in sensitive regions, and the implementation of strategic projects that do not depend on market forces. In accounting terms, they generate less value than private firms; in political terms, they generate stability. They are the organs through which the centre exercises granular control over the territory, manages crises, and implements countercyclical policies. In many phases, SOEs have functioned as shock absorbers: absorbing surplus labour, building infrastructure not always needed, ensuring that the economy did not derail when the private sector slowed. Their rationale is not economic; it is political. That is why they endure —and why they are central.

Beside the SOEs, and often displaying surprising dynamism, stand China's major private groups—technology, manufacturing, logistics, finance. They have generated the visible innovation and turned China into a laboratory of technological experimentation. But their role is not autonomous. The private sector in China is neither a counterpower nor an independent actor. It is a productive force that prospers only insofar as it remains within the political perimeter drawn by the centre. Its freedom is wide in practice, narrow in principle. It may innovate, invest, expand globally; but it cannot contradict the system's fundamental logic: a political authority that tolerates no external competition and no alternative centres of influence. A large private firm can become an economic engine, but it cannot become a political actor. Whenever the two dimensions begin to overlap, the centre intervenes.

Recent history makes this point unmistakably clear. The technology sector, celebrated for years as the symbol of China's modernisation, suddenly became the terrain of political disciplining. Firms that had accumulated too much public trust, too much capital, too much informational power were cut down through rapid and pervasive regulatory campaigns. This was not merely a market correction; it was a reassertion of political order. The lesson is simple: a firm's economic magnitude does not determine its fate—its position within the political bloc does. China does not know the separation of powers; it knows the separation of tasks. Private firms are free to create value, but not free to create power.

Within this system, "political alignment" is not an exceptional act but the everyday norm. It means accepting that corporate strategy must be compatible with Party guidelines; that internal governance must reflect the presence of political cells; that public communication must avoid any gesture that could be interpreted as ideological autonomy. State-owned or private, all firms share a single principle: survival depends on the ability to interpret political signals correctly. This is not a regime of terror; it is a regime of anticipation. Politics does not intervene constantly, but it *can* intervene—and that possibility alone is enough to shape behaviour.

From this dynamic emerges what we might call a block economy: every sector is a bloc, every bloc has a political centre of reference, every centre delineates the actors' room for manoeuvre. The boundaries are not economic but ideological. Competition exists and can be intense, but it remains contained within limits that must not be crossed. Private firms do not compete with the state; they compete with one another to interpret the state's logic as faithfully as possible.

This structure explains both China's success and its fragility. Its success lies in political alignment, which allows the government to mobilise resources quickly, avoid institutional deadlock, and steer capital towards national objectives. Its fragility lies in the same logic, which prevents the emergence of counterpowers, oversight mechanisms, and channels of internal critique. China is a system that works as long as the central leadership maintains the right balance between impulse and restraint; when that balance breaks, the entire bloc stiffens or contracts. Jin describes an ecosystem in which state and market cooperate; in reality, it is an ecosystem in which the market prospers when power allows it—and shrinks whenever power decides to redefine the perimeter of the possible.

In its deepest structure, the Chinese economy is not a sum of state and private enterprises but a single organism articulated into blocs that all respond—directly or indirectly—to the same logic: politics as the ultimate criterion of legitimacy. Those who fail to integrate this into their analysis cannot understand China. Those who, like Jin, leave politics at the margins of the picture end up producing a brilliant but partial image—an elegant conceptual architecture that collapses as soon as one moves from abstraction to the real functioning of the system.

WHERE JIN IS RIGHT: WHAT THE WEST HAS ALWAYS UNDERESTIMATED

If Jin is often indulgent toward the Chinese system and at times blind to its structural risks, she nonetheless has the merit of emphasising several points that the West has systematically misunderstood. These insights do not absolve the model, but they make it more legible; and, above all, they reveal how deeply our own perspective is conditioned by political and moral categories that do not always illuminate. On these points, Jin is not merely correct—she reflects back to the West an image of its own limitations.

The first element the West has underestimated is China's capacity for institutional learning. Despite opacity, despite political rigidity, despite the absence of checks and balances, the Party has shown remarkable ability in reforming what did not work, in altering course when an entire historical phase proved untenable, in reassembling parts of the system with a pragmatism free of ideology. This does not mean it always did so well, nor that it will continue to do so, but the Western idea of an immobile monolith is simply false. China has moved through cycles of opening and closure, has tested local models before generalising them, has radically shifted its industrial strategies. It is not a state that learns as a democracy learns—because it cannot do so through public conflict or transparency—but it learns nonetheless: through administrative trial and error, through obsessive observation of outcomes, through the centralised management of success and failure. The West has often mistaken this adaptive capacity for ruthless authoritarianism, or it has failed to perceive it altogether because it did not know where to look.

The second underestimated element is the real weight of internal competition in China—not political competition, which is absent, but economic and administrative competition. For decades, Chinese cities did not compete in the name of pluralism; they competed to remain visible to the centre, to attract investment, to demonstrate efficiency, to climb the Party hierarchy. This competition was a powerful engine—one that no Western observer anticipated in the 1980s, when China seemed condemned to a kind of 1950s stagnation. The idea that an authoritarian system could generate such fierce economic rivalry appeared self-contradictory. It was not. China demonstrated that competitive dynamics can arise not only from markets but from the combination of political incentives and administrative pressure. It is a form of competition different from that of the West —faster, more imitative, more unrestrained—but no less effective. Jin captures this phenomenon with precision, and she is right to highlight it.

The third point concerns the role of private entrepreneurship, which the West has often misconstrued under the image of a state-dominated economy. The mistake is twofold: the West has overestimated the centrality of state-owned firms and underestimated the creative energy of the private sector. For many analysts, China in the 2000s was a country producing imitations and cheap goods; few realised that Chinese digital platforms were innovating business models that the West would only imitate years later. Integrated logistics, "horizontal" e-commerce, the evolution of digital payments, the speed of technological iteration—none of these emerged from SOEs; they arose in the private market. Here Jin is not only right; she states a truth many Western economists ignored out of ideological prejudice. China did not become competitive because it "exploited labour," but because it allowed a frontier capitalism to grow within a framework of political discipline.

This leads to the fourth point: social cohesion as an economic resource. The West often interprets Chinese stability as the product of repression. Jin reminds us that a cultural code also exists—one made of patience, collective aspiration for improvement, respect for authority—that enabled a transformation which elsewhere would have produced constant unrest. For better or worse, part of the Chinese population accepted enormous sacrifices not only because they were forced to, but because they believed collective growth would bring real benefits. The Western error here was double: first to deny this cohesion, then to romanticise it. Jin has the merit of restoring it to a concrete level—as a sociological factor, not an ideological one. It can create stability, but it can also generate resignation. It can be a strength, but also a limit. Still, it exists, and ignoring it means failing to understand China.

Finally, Jin is right to remind readers that the West has overestimated itself as a universal model. For decades, the implicit thesis was that economic modernisation would inevitably push China toward a liberal political model. This thesis proved unfounded. China has shown that it is possible to industrialise, innovate, and become a technological power without adopting liberal democracy. This is a fact, not a value judgement. The West did not foresee it because it confused a normative desire with a historical law. Jin is right to unmask this error—not to celebrate authoritarianism, but to remind us that history has no predetermined direction. Here too, her realism is an antidote to the teleology through which we often read the global story.

In all these insights, Jin does not construct an apology for China; she dismantles an apology for the West. And that is perhaps her strongest contribution: she forces us to see China not as a distorted mirror of our own model, but as an autonomous historical object with its own logics and compromises. What the West has underestimated is not the virtues of the Party, but the sheer power of the social and economic forces China has mobilised. To understand the fragility of the Chinese model—and that will be the next step—we must first recognise what made its rise possible. On this point Jin provides a valuable foundation; the problem lies in everything she chooses not to see.

PART II

THE CHINESE MODEL UNDER THE TEST OF REALITY

The Hidden Fragility: Debt, "Cathedrals in the Desert," and Stimulated Growth

LOCAL GOVERNMENTS FINANCING VEHICLES (LGFV)

To identify the exact point at which the Chinese "miracle" begins to waver, one must look not at the major state-owned enterprises nor at the private tech giants, but at the seemingly invisible level of local governments. It is there that we find the mechanism which, for decades, fuelled growth and now threatens it: the Local Governments Financing Vehicles (LGFV). These are shell companies created by local administrations to bypass formal borrowing limits and finance investments that—on paper—were meant to transform China into a flawless modernity of highways, bridges, industrial zones, and futuristic urban districts. In practice, they have generated one of the largest debt bubbles in history.

LGFVs are the dark heart of Chinese decentralisation. Because local governments cannot issue debt directly, they created thousands of semi-public entities to take out loans using the rising value of urbanisable land as collateral. The model seemed perfect: the city grows, land values rise, LGFVs easily secure financing, and the infrastructure they build generates new economic activity. The cycle feeds itself and produces exactly what the political centre wants: rapid growth, urbanisation, visible results. For years, it was the backbone of the Chinese boom. But the mechanism contained an original flaw: it assumed that real-estate demand and territorial expansion could continue indefinitely.

LGFV debt grew at a vertiginous pace, reaching levels that today escape all statistical transparency. It is not "public debt" in the traditional sense, nor is it "private debt": it is systemic debt, involving banks, local governments, construction firms, and households. And this debt did not finance only useful infrastructure—it financed hundreds of unnecessary projects, industrial zones with no firms, roads with no traffic, residential districts with no residents. The infamous "ghost cities" are not a folkloric anomaly but the structural sign of an economy that has confused quantity with quality, expansion with development, investment with productivity.

The logic behind this mechanism is the same logic Jin celebrates as local dynamism: officials whose careers depend on indicators; public and private firms eager to participate in the immense construction spiral; banks lending freely because they know they are implicitly or explicitly backed by political power. Each actor behaved rationally within the system—but the system as a whole became irrational. This is the point Jin does not see: what appears as individual merit produces, in the aggregate, collective risk.

LGFVs, long celebrated as instruments of modernisation, are now the great taboo of Chinese economic discourse. No one can afford to acknowledge the true scale of the debt, because doing so would undermine the narrative of stability. But the fact is undeniable: a significant portion of the resources invested in the last two decades has not generated adequate returns. It has generated only accounting growth. If China achieved spectacular growth rates, it owes much to this hidden debt that artificially boosted the economy, pushing the cost of correction ever further into the future.

The paradox is that this system—seemingly functional for many years—now traps China precisely where it sought to free itself: in structural dependence on real estate and infrastructure investment. LGFVs physically built the country, but they eroded its financial foundations. Today, many of these entities are unable to repay their debts: they survive only through continuous rollovers, new loans to cover old ones. The risk is clear: a prolonged slowdown, a crisis of confidence in local credit markets, a mix of financial and political fragility that no technical intervention can resolve quickly.

Here Jin's narrative breaks down. Administrative capacity, local dynamism, internal competition—the pillars of her model—are the same factors that fuelled an uncontrollable debt spiral. What was a virtue in an expansionary phase becomes a vice in a mature economy. China today needs a new model, but LGFVs keep it tied to the old one; it needs productivity, but LGFVs have produced concrete and steel; it needs transparency, but LGFVs operate in opacity.

This is the hidden fragility of the Chinese miracle: not a marginal mistake, not a historical accident, but the logical consequence of the way China engineered its development. And the fact that Jin does not confront this issue is not a casual omission: it is the symptom of how deeply the official narrative continues to confuse efficiency with accumulation, growth with debt, modernisation with accounting illusion.

We continue from here.

INFRASTRUCTURE THAT CREATES NO VALUE

In the official narrative—and in the reading Jin tends to adopt—infrastructure is the emblem of Chinese efficiency: bridges spanning vast territories, highways stitching together newly invented cities, high-speed rail lines extending like arteries of a growing organism. The West, entangled in permits, appeals, and bureaucratic paralysis, looks at this capacity with a mixture of envy and disbelief. Yet it is precisely the infrastructure sector that reveals, more than any other, the ambivalent and in many ways unsustainable nature of China's development: an extraordinary executive power that has produced, alongside genuinely useful works, an enormous mass of investments devoid of real economic value. These are the infrastructures that generate no value—the physical counterpart to the invisible debt accumulated by local governments.

For years, the logic was simple, almost mechanical: to build was to grow. Every new road added to GDP; every bridge enhanced the political visibility of a local leader; every urban district was tangible proof of progress underway. The incentive system—built around local GDP as the primary metric of evaluation—pushed generations of officials to prioritise quantity over the actual needs of their territories. In many regions, especially in the country's interior, industrial zones without firms proliferated, residential complexes remained half-empty, airports were built only a few years apart, dams and expressways were oversized relative to demand. At times these projects served geopolitical or strategic purposes; far more often they were the materialisation of an uncontrolled administrative impulse, fuelled by easy credit and by internal competition that rewarded what appeared, not what endured.

The fundamental point—one Jin touches on only in passing—is that much of this infrastructure generates no economic return. A road linking two non-existent industrial districts does not create traffic; an airport built to serve an imagined tourist market does not sell tickets; a cluster of skyscrapers erected in a city that is not growing generates neither urban life nor real-estate value. And yet, at the moment of their construction, all these works inflated GDP, stimulated credit, and created temporary employment. It is the paradigm of the "cathedral in the desert": a costly, imposing, often technologically advanced structure that remains isolated in a context that has no use for it. In the West, such projects become scandals; in China, they were for decades an integral part of the model.

These non-productive infrastructures create a double distortion. The first is economic: they represent immobilised capital without generating cash flows to repay the debt incurred to build them. They become permanent liabilities, concealed in local budgets through accounting tricks, shell companies, and continual debt rollovers. The second distortion is political: they create the illusion of attained modernity, of linear progress, while in reality hiding structural fragilities that no government wishes to confront openly. On official maps, new infrastructures appear as symbols of a rising power; in everyday reality, many of them deteriorate without ever having been truly used.

It is crucial to understand the internal logic of this phenomenon. Jin tends to interpret the emphasis on infrastructure as proof of the state's capacity to coordinate and mobilise resources, but the truth is more complex. LGFVs needed to build incessantly because their financing model relied on the continuous appreciation of land values. If a local government stops building, it stops generating the real-estate value that supports its debt. Infrastructure growth was not an act of vision but a bookkeeping necessity: provincial economies could not slow down, because slowing down would have exposed the losses. This does not erase the fact that many infrastructures improved the lives of millions; but a significant portion arose not from genuine need, but from the pressure to keep the debt cycle running.

The deeper consequence is that China has invested enormous quantities of resources—material, environmental, financial—into projects that do not raise long-term productivity. And a country that invests heavily without increasing productivity accelerates its own fragility. In other words: China has built more than its economy could sustain, more than its cities could absorb, more than its population could use. This is the dark side of a system in which decision-making speed can turn myopic. Speed that, when not accompanied by critical evaluation, produces waste, debt, territorial inequality, and a landscape of structures that create no value.

This phenomenon is not a marginal anomaly but a structural trajectory of Chinese development: it is the price of a model that has prioritised rapid growth over sustainable growth, visibility over returns, the expansion of numbers over the health of real economic fundamentals. Jin admires China's capacity to build; what she does not see is that building, in China, has too often been synonymous with the need to continue building—simply to prevent the very architecture of the economy from revealing its cracks. Apparent efficiency here is the other face of immense dissipation.

WHY CHINA HAS STOPPED GROWING AS BEFORE (AND WHY JIN DOES NOT SAY SO)

To understand why China has stopped growing as it once did, one must set aside both the West's catastrophic prophecies and the narrative optimism that Jin, consciously or not, continues to endorse. China has not fallen into crisis overnight, nor is it the victim of an external fate: it is simply reaching the structural limits of the model that propelled it forward at unprecedented speed. These limits were embedded in the model from the start, but as long as the scale of expansion was vast and the population young and mobile, they remained invisible. Today, they emerge with clarity. The slowdown is not an accident: it is the natural manifestation of a cycle that could not last indefinitely. And it is precisely here that Jin's reading loses contact with reality: she does not acknowledge that the very successes she celebrates are the same forces now constraining the country.

The first limit is the law of diminishing marginal productivity. For nearly thirty years, China grew by shifting labour from the countryside to the city, from ultra-low-productivity activities to rapidly expanding industries. It was a massive and easy leap: every worker transferred generated an immediate rise in average productivity. But this process, by its nature, cannot continue forever. Once hundreds of millions have been urbanised, the marginal gain of each new transfer declines. Urbanisation is no longer enough: innovation becomes necessary. And innovation is a process very different from building factories or infrastructure: it requires institutions, freedom to experiment, informational transparency, tolerance for failure. All conditions that an increasingly centralised political system struggles to provide.

The second limit is the saturation of the infrastructure model. China has built more, and faster, than any other economy in history. But an infrastructure—road, bridge, railway—has economic meaning only if it generates value for decades. Chinese infrastructure often generated accounting growth at the moment of construction but does not always generate real value in subsequent years. When an economy keeps investing in projects that do not yield returns, aggregate productivity stalls. And indeed China's Total Factor Productivity (TFP) has been stagnant for more than a decade. Jin does not state this clearly, because it undermines her thesis of a self-correcting state. Yet it is a fact: China grows more slowly because it channels ever more capital into sectors that do not increase productivity.

The third limit is debt. The combination of hidden public debt (chiefly local), real-estate debt, and SOE debt has reached levels that make it impossible to continue stimulating the economy with further capital injections. As long as growth rates were in the double digits, repaying debt was relatively easy: wealth creation exceeded costs. But once growth slowed, the debt became unsustainable. It is like a machine designed to function only at high speed: when it decelerates, it vibrates, breaks down, wears out. Jin is very attentive to China's financial capacity, far less attentive to the fragility accumulated over time. The result is a narrative that ignores the systemic risk of a model that postponed its reckoning for years.

The fourth limit is demography. Population ageing—accelerated by the one-child policy and the social costs of urban life—is shrinking not only the labour force but also the base of consumers, innovators, and young entrepreneurs. China does not simply have fewer children: it has fewer young families willing to take risks, less spontaneous social mobility, less demographic energy to support an intensive growth model. In the West, this phenomenon is often dismissed as a pension issue; in China, it is a structural problem of the development model. A country that grows by moving masses of young people into new cities cannot continue to grow once that youthful mass no longer exists. Jin acknowledges demography as a challenge but underestimates its systemic scope.

The fifth limit is what one might call the political paradox of innovation. Innovation requires the freedom to explore, to err, to defy the status quo. But a political system that over the last decade has increased control, centralised power, disciplined major private firms, and reinforced ideological apparatuses does not create an environment conducive to creativity. China still has extraordinary innovators and competitive technological sectors, but frontier innovation requires a political climate that does not punish deviation, does not fear novelty, does not perceive private success as a potential threat to central authority. This is where the model slows: the logic of political alignment—which worked for investment and physical construction—works far less when the task is to generate new ideas.

The sixth limit is the loss of household confidence. China grew at dizzying rates also because families believed in the promise of the future: work hard, save, buy a home, secure a better life for one's children. Today that promise has cracked. The real-estate market is in crisis, social mobility is slowing, political uncertainty is rising, and social and psychological pressure are greater than ever. Chinese society has not collapsed—but it has stopped running. And an economy built on permanent acceleration cannot withstand a slowdown in collective aspiration.

Jin does not deny all this explicitly; she simply does not engage with it. She prefers to interpret the slowdown as a temporary phase, a necessary adjustment, a transition toward a different economic maturity. And to some extent this is true: all mature economies slow down. But China is not facing only the physiological deceleration of an economy that has already harvested the gains of industrialisation; it is confronting the intrinsic limits of a model that built its strength on speed, mobilisation, debt, and favourable demography.

Chinese growth is not over. But China will never grow as it once did. And the reason is not contingent; it is structural. Everything that made China great is now making it fragile. Jin recounts the bright side of the model; what is missing from her analysis is the shadow that inevitably grows when a great acceleration reaches the end of its historical cycle. We will continue to trace its consequences.

The Demographic Knot: A Century Without Youth

THE GREATEST PEACE-TIME DEMOGRAPHIC COLLAPSE IN HISTORY

Among all the forces that will shape China's future, none is more decisive—or more inexorable—than its demographic decline. The numbers are well known, yet their historical magnitude is rarely grasped: China is undergoing the greatest demographic collapse ever experienced by a nation in peacetime. No war, no famine, no pandemic has had an impact comparable to the one produced by the combination of ultra-low birth rates, rapid ageing, and the structural imbalances created by decades of family-planning policies. It is a silent transition, but one of systemic violence—something no economic model can absorb without profound consequences.

The shrinking of the population is not an episodic phenomenon; it is now an irreversible trend. Having reached its peak, China's population will begin contracting at an increasingly rapid pace, following a trajectory reminiscent of Japan's—but on a vastly larger scale. Within a few generations, China may lose hundreds of millions of inhabitants. This is not alarmism; it is arithmetic. The fertility rate—officially around 1.0, but likely even lower in urban areas—is among the lowest in the world. A country that for millennia grounded its strength in sheer demographic abundance now faces a horizon in which the elderly will vastly outnumber the young.

This decline is not only numerical but qualitative. For decades, China enjoyed a unique "demographic dividend": an immense mass of young, mobile, disciplined, aspirational workers. They were the true engine of development, far more than five-year plans or state enterprises. Modernisation passed through the bodies of a generation that accepted enormous sacrifices, radical geographic displacement, relentless work rhythms, and unceasing educational and professional competition. That engine no longer exists. The country no longer has an unlimited labour force to mobilise, nor a vast cohort of youth ready to sustain urbanisation and industrial expansion. China thus enters a new phase, in which growth can no longer be driven by demography but must depend on productivity and innovation—two domains in which political pressure and ideological tightening do not always foster the necessary boldness.

The collapse in birth rates has been exacerbated by the soaring cost of urban life. Unlike Japan or South Korea, where families often forgo children by choice or due to existential pessimism, China's phenomenon also has a deeper structural root: the prohibitive cost of education. Educational competition—the direct offspring of the meritocratic policies Jin praises—has become both a psychological and financial barrier. Having a child means taking on the weight of an entire system of expectations, investments, and anxieties. The urban generation born in the 1990s and 2000s—supposed to embody the country's new demographic energy—feels instead that it lives in an environment too rigid, too expensive, too competitive to afford the "luxury" of multiple children. And when a society loses its hope in children, the problem is no longer statistical: it is the sign of a spiritual shift.

Ageing is the other face of the same problem. Millions of Chinese are entering retirement without a robust pension system and without younger generations numerous enough to support them fiscally. The traditional family structure—once the universal shock absorber of hardship—is crumbling under the weight of urban mobility. Young people no longer live with their parents; grandparents can no longer live near grandchildren; families have shrunk to two- or three-person units unable to absorb collective shocks. The result is a country in which intergenerational solidarity weakens just as the need for care expands. The healthcare system, already strained, will soon face the pressure of millions of chronically ill, non-self-sufficient elderly. China has built futuristic cities, but it has not built a welfare state adequate for the age that awaits it.

This picture clarifies why Jin's narrative feels incomplete. In her account, China is still a young, dynamic country driven by the energy of a cohesive society willing to sacrifice for the common good. But that vision belongs to the 2000s, not to the present. Today's China is a nation ageing faster than any great power in history, and one that is losing its primary resource: youth in abundance. This is not a temporary constraint nor an obstacle to be solved through clever policies; it is a structural fact that will irreversibly reshape the economic, social, and psychological trajectory of the nation. Until Jin integrates this reality fully into her analysis, her narrative remains anchored to a world that no longer exists.

China's future is a future with fewer workers, fewer taxpayers, fewer young families, less aspirational momentum. A future in which growth will necessarily be slower, more difficult, more dependent on innovations requiring freedom and pluralism—precisely what the political system now tends to compress. This does not mean China will decline; it means that the historical cycle that made it great has run its course. Anyone seeking to understand the Chinese model as it confronts reality must start here: with the absence of what was once abundant. A century without youth is a century that demands of China a new economic language—and perhaps, too, a new political one.

IMPACT ON LABOUR, PRODUCTIVITY, WELFARE, AND INNOVATION

China's demographic decline is not an external variable to the economic system but its new gravitational force: everything, in the coming decades, will have to revolve around the scarcity of youth and the abundance of the elderly. The consequences extend across four domains—labour, productivity, welfare, and innovation—and they are so profound that they call into question the very foundations of the development model China has followed until now. Here Jin's narrative definitively loses contact with reality: she describes a country that can still rely on the same human resources and the same modernising impulse that powered it for decades, when in fact the historical ground has shifted radically.

On the labour front, China is entering an entirely new phase. For forty years the labour supply was inexhaustible: every factory, every industrial zone, every new productive sector could immediately find millions of young workers ready to fill the jobs. This is no longer the case. The reservoir of young labour is drying up, along with the advantage that sustained China's competitiveness: low wages, worker abundance, and the ability to reassign labour across sectors with extreme flexibility. Today many factories report staff shortages; some regions offer even modest incentives just to attract workers. The bargaining power of the young is rising—not because civil society has become stronger, but because young people are simply fewer. The result is twofold: wages rise (good for workers, less good for labour-intensive firms), and many labour-based industries risk losing competitiveness, accelerating the shift toward automation. It is the end of the "China as the world's factory" model.

On productivity, the dynamic is even more critical. An ageing society not only shrinks the labour force; it makes it less flexible, less mobile, less willing to change sectors or relocate. The great internal migrations that fuelled urbanisation for decades will not occur again: young people are fewer and more educated, and they will not accept the material conditions that the previous generation endured. Productivity rises when a society can rapidly reassign human and physical capital; when structures harden, every shock produces less innovation and more stagnation. Moreover, the decline in youth reduces the share of workers in the most dynamic age group—the cohort that statistically creates more new firms, more patents, more technological shifts. Demography thus begins to turn into destiny: China risks falling into the "middle-growth trap," where ever greater investment yields ever smaller returns.

The third impact concerns welfare, which in China remains a patchwork of incomplete, unequal, and underfunded systems. As long as the population was young, it was relatively easy to support the elderly with moderate contributions and a still-strong family network. But today each young person must support two parents and four grandparents; and many must do so alone, because fertility has fallen so low that the traditional mechanism of familial mutual aid has collapsed. The healthcare system is under strain, and will be increasingly so: chronic illnesses, rapid ageing, rising care costs. The pension system is unprepared: contributions will not be sufficient to sustain a rapidly expanding elderly population. For the first time in modern history, China will have to build a welfare state not out of prosperity but out of slowdown. And here the model encounters a profound limit: a modern welfare state requires transparency, public trust, stable fiscal resources, and an administrative apparatus oriented not toward growth but toward social protection. This is a cultural and political shift the Party has not yet begun to undertake.

The fourth impact—perhaps the most decisive—concerns innovation. Every country that has thrived in the knowledge economy has done so thanks to demographic vitality: young people who take risks, experiment, launch companies, break patterns. It is no coincidence that major innovation hubs—Silicon Valley, Israel, South Korea in the 1990s—emerged in young, expanding societies. China, by contrast, is entering a phase in which its youth population is not only shrinking but also becoming more risk-averse, more focused on personal stability, more suffocated by an extremely selective and competitive educational system. Add to this the political tightening of recent years, and the picture is clear: China seeks to innovate in an environment that discourages heterodoxy. Innovation is still possible—China retains enormous scientific and technological resources—but it becomes structurally more difficult. Demography acts as an invisible brake: it reduces the margin for error, raises the cost of experimentation, and lowers the capacity to generate "creative ecosystems."

In sum, the demographic knot is not one problem among others: it is the matrix from which all other problems derive. A rapidly ageing country must reinvent its development model, and China does not yet seem to have accepted this necessity. Jin, in her analysis, tends to minimise this impact or treat it as a challenge manageable through industrial policy and fertility incentives. But the truth is that no policy can swiftly reverse a demographic decline already deeply rooted, and no economic reform can compensate for the disappearance of entire generations.

China will enter the future with fewer workers, fewer consumers, fewer innovators; with more retirees, more chronic illnesses, more economic rigidity. It is an epochal transition that no optimistic narrative can avoid. Anyone seeking to understand China's future must begin here: with a nation that, for the first time in its millennia-long history, must learn to live not in expansion but in contraction. And this lesson, still, is absent from Jin's account.

JIN'S THESIS ON "SOCIAL RESILIENCE": WHY IT ISN'T ENOUGH

One of the strongest—and most appealing—elements in Jin's narrative is what she calls China's social resilience: the collective capacity to endure hardship, adapt rapidly to change, and maintain cohesion even in the face of economic or political difficulty. According to Jin, it is this resilience that allowed China to modernise without uncontrolled fractures, to avoid the chaos the West expected, and to withstand waves of urbanisation, radical reforms, sectoral crises, and even the pandemic without collapsing. It is a powerful argument: China would not only be a disciplined country, but one capable of absorbing shocks better than any industrial democracy.

And yet this thesis, although it contains a kernel of truth, is no longer sufficient to explain the historical phase China is entering today. Not because resilience has disappeared—much of it still exists—but because the nature of the shocks has changed. They are no longer external or cyclical shocks, but structural ones: they concern demography, debt, stagnant productivity, and the slowing of social mobility. These are forces that operate over the long term, corroding precisely what once made that resilience possible. Jin's argument assumes that Chinese society is still willing to make sacrifices similar to those of previous generations, but that assumption is no longer guaranteed.

The first limit of Chinese resilience is that it is not an infinite resource. It was built over time on an implicit pact: growth in exchange for stability. People accepted extreme work rhythms, territorial inequalities, and weak social protections because they saw a clear trajectory of material improvement ahead. That pact is now beginning to fray. Economic prospects are less certain, the housing market no longer offers guarantees, jobs are harder to find for young people, and the very idea of linear progress has weakened. Resilience based on the promise of upward mobility loses strength when that mobility slows. One cannot ask the generations born in the 2000s for the same sacrifices made by those born in the 1960s or 1980s: they do not face the same horizon.

The second limit concerns the changing nature of social pressure. Chinese resilience was never just about endurance; it was also a way of internalising a collective duty in pursuit of a better future. But today that pressure has reversed direction: it no longer pushes toward achieving new prosperity but toward maintaining a fragile status in a hyper-competitive society. Youth depression, the lying-flat movement, growing aversion to entrepreneurial risk, and overwhelming academic anxiety are not signs of resilience—they are signs of a population that can no longer transform pressure into energy. What Jin interprets as resilience risks being, for the younger generations, a mixture of disillusionment and passive adaptation.

The third limit concerns the relationship between resilience and innovation. China was resilient during a phase of extensive growth—that is, growth based on the continual accumulation of resources, labour, and investment. But now it needs intensive innovation: new ideas, new firms, new frontier technologies. Resilience, in this context, can become an obstacle: a system that is too cohesive, too oriented toward obedience, too preoccupied with stability tends to penalise non-conformists—those who fail, who experiment, who break patterns. The resilience Jin celebrates is an "orderly," disciplined resilience; but innovation requires a "creative" resilience, which the current political climate struggles to tolerate. Resilience alone is not enough: one must also be free to experiment, and today's China offers far narrower spaces than it did a decade ago.

The fourth limit is the politicisation of resilience itself. Resilience has become a rhetorical tool of official propaganda: a way to praise the nation's capacity to overcome obstacles and to justify calls for continual sacrifice. This risks turning resilience into an imposed virtue rather than a chosen one. A society may accept being resilient in the face of a crisis; accepting it as a permanent condition is another matter. Here Jin's narrative reveals its fragility: she assumes resilience is an almost natural constant of Chinese society, when in reality it was the product of specific historical conditions that are now rapidly changing.

The fifth limit concerns the growing deficit of trust. Social resilience cannot indefinitely compensate for declining confidence in the future, in institutions, or in the economy. And a country that is ageing rapidly, heavily indebted, and facing a more uncertain labour market tends naturally toward distrust. Families save more because they fear uncertainty; they reduce consumption because they see little growth ahead; they avoid having children because they perceive few guarantees. Here too, resilience is not an antidote: it can delay the emergence of problems, but it cannot eliminate them.

Chinese social resilience is real, but it is a historical phenomenon, not a permanent attribute. It functioned in an era when society was growing, the economy was expanding, and mobility was tangible. Today, in an era of demographic contraction, economic slowdown, increasing political control, and social fatigue, that same resilience risks turning into passive adaptation or resignation.

This is what Jin fails to see: resilience is not an eternal capital. It is a credit the Party received from society, and one that is now beginning to be consumed. To confront the new structural challenges, something else will be required—not only resilience but creative freedom, new ideas, economic and social pluralism. And the central question, which will accompany the rest of this book, is whether China's political system is capable of producing or even tolerating these resources.

True Innovation or Effective Imitation?

CHINA'S R&D BOOM: LIGHT AND SHADOW

At first glance, China appears to have already won the innovation race. In every strategic sector—artificial intelligence, 5G, electric vehicles, biotechnology, photovoltaics, robotics—its investments are staggering, scientific publications are rising, and patents are multiplying. Statistics depict an apparently straightforward story: a country investing more than any other, producing more engineering doctorates, and graduating millions of STEM students every year. Jin takes these indicators as proof that China has already made the transition from imitator to innovator, and that its historical lag behind the West is now a thing of the past.

But this reading is incomplete. China's apparent explosion of innovation masks a far more uneven landscape—one made of concentrated excellence, large-scale attempts, massive duplication, investments that do not always generate new knowledge, and a political structure still struggling to produce the conditions needed for frontier innovation. To understand China, one must distinguish between *true* innovation and *effective imitation*: two phenomena that coexist, but are not the same.

On the one hand, it is undeniable that China has achieved extraordinary progress in large-scale imitation. It has perfected a model found nowhere else: replicating mature technologies, improving them rapidly, lowering their cost, and overtaking competitors through a colossal industrial system, a highly specialised workforce, and massive state support. This is how the country became a global leader in solar panels, electric vehicles, batteries, drones, and advanced telecommunications. Here China is not simply a "copycat": it is a powerhouse of optimisation. It takes what works and makes it faster, cheaper, more scalable. This is not a limitation—it is a formidable industrial talent that the West has consistently underestimated.

On the other hand, original innovation—the kind that springs from fundamental research, unfocused exploration, intellectual audacity—remains less solid than Jin suggests. China produces an enormous volume of scientific articles, but average quality varies widely; it generates vast numbers of patents, but many are incremental or duplicated; its R&D spending is immense, but often channelled into top-down projects where success is rewarded more than discovery and failure is barely tolerated. This does not mean that brilliant innovators are lacking—far from it—and in certain sectors China is already at the frontier. But the system as a whole does not yet produce the cultural ecosystem that turns innovation into a continuous, independent, unpredictable cycle.

The central issue is exactly this: China excels at *directed, planned, strategic* innovation; it struggles with *emergent*, *spontaneous*, *non-programmable* innovation. This structural limitation stems from three factors.

First, political pressure. In recent years, increased centralisation of power and heightened ideological control have made it harder for students, researchers, and entrepreneurs to take real risks. Innovation does not arise from obedience but from heterodoxy; not from respect for authority but from the freedom to deviate. In a system where political security takes precedence over creativity, where major tech firms have been forcefully disciplined, where private success is often perceived as a potential threat to the centre, spontaneous innovation shrinks. Jin completely overlooks this effect—and unsurprisingly so, as it is where economics and politics collide most painfully.

Second, the structure of scientific incentives. China invests heavily in applied research, but fundamental research remains fragile. Universities and research institutes often operate like bureaucratic apparatuses: publication counts, formal awards, official recognition. This model produces quantity, not originality; application, not paradigm shifts. Scientific revolutions do not follow five-year plans—they emerge from free minds working in environments that embrace unpredictability. China excels when goals are clear and measurable; it struggles when they cannot be defined in advance.

Third, the limited mobility of creative human capital. China's most talented young scholars can obtain extraordinary opportunities in Western universities or companies, where they enjoy greater freedom of inquiry and fewer political constraints. China tries to retain them or lure them back, but it faces a cultural reality: innovation thrives where innovators *want* to live, not where the state wishes to place them. Funding laboratories is not enough; one must create living environments where thought is unafraid. This is one of the least discussed limits of the Chinese model today.

Yet it would be a mistake to underestimate China: its industrial capacity, speed of applied learning, and technological infrastructure surpass those of many Western countries. Effective imitation is already a form of power. But unless China resolves the tension between political control and intellectual freedom, its innovation will remain incomplete. This is not an ideological argument; it is a historical law: great waves of creativity do not arise in systems that fear the unexpected.

Jin portrays a China ready to lead the next scientific revolution. The truth is more complex: China *is* ready—but its political system is not. Innovation is an act of trust in uncertainty, and contemporary China is a country trying, in every sphere, to minimise uncertainty. This tension will be decisive for its technological future.

THE THIN LINE BETWEEN CATCH-UP AND RADICAL INNOVATION

To understand the nature of Chinese innovation, one must distinguish between two historical phases: the *catch-up phase*, in which a country rapidly closes the gap separating it from advanced economies, and the *radical innovation phase*, in which a country not only narrows that gap but positions itself at the frontier of knowledge, generating discoveries the world has never seen. Jin tends to treat these two phases as if they were a natural continuation of one another—almost an inevitable progression: after imitation, innovation; after copying, creation. But economic history shows the opposite: the transition from catch-up to radical innovation is neither automatic, nor guaranteed, nor common. It is a leap that requires institutional, social, cultural, and psychological conditions profoundly different from those that drive catch-up.

China has excelled at catch-up. It industrialised entire sectors within a few years, absorbed foreign technologies with remarkable speed, climbed global value chains, and turned imported ideas into efficient, improved, affordable products. This process requires organisation, discipline, coordination, capital, and abundant labour—all resources that China has mobilised with extraordinary cohesion. But catch-up, by definition, is a reactive process: one learns what others have invented, optimises what others have designed, scales what others have already tested. It is creative imitation, yes, but still imitation.

Radical innovation is something else entirely. It requires not only resources; it requires *freedom.* Intellectual freedom, social freedom, economic freedom. It requires error, competing ideas, visible failure, fearless criticism, and a culture that rewards deviation more than conformity—one that sees potential in wild ideas rather than threats. This kind of innovation emerges where control is limited, not where it is pervasive; where politics accepts unpredictability, not where it seeks to neutralise it in advance. Here the Chinese model reveals its limits, and Jin's narrative—presuming continuity between imitation and innovation—obscures a fundamental discontinuity.

The problem is not that China is incapable of radical innovation. There are sectors—aerospace, quantum communications, supercomputing, certain areas of artificial intelligence—in which China is not merely catching up but creating new paths. But these islands of advanced innovation coexist with vast archipelagos of incremental research, duplication, and forced investment. They are exceptions, not yet the rule.

The boundary between catch-up and radical innovation is thin because it is psychological before it is technical. A country accustomed to growing by imitating what works must learn to tolerate what does *not* yet work; it must accept confusion, failure, the chaotic freedom of scientific exploration. Radical innovation is a constant rupture with the existing order. It requires a culture unafraid of individualism, one that rewards iconoclasts and does not punish those who question what is taken for granted. This is where China pays the price of its own stability. The current political system prioritises order, predictability, discipline. But radical innovation is disorder, unpredictability, creative indiscipline.

Jin interprets the country's scientific energy as proof that the transition has already occurred. In reality, what we see is a system in incomplete transition: China has developed extraordinary capacity to reproduce and improve what it already knows, but it has not yet created the conditions to produce what it *does not* know. The risk is not total stagnation—China is too large, too competent, too interconnected to stop innovating—but asymmetric innovation: advanced in a handful of strategic sectors, weak in the broader landscape of research.

The line separating catch-up from radical innovation is also a political line. As long as the Party's priority remains control, and as long as ideological alignment remains the condition for access to resources, China will be able to imitate better than anyone, to apply faster than anyone, to industrialise technologies more rapidly than anyone—but it will not be able to innovate more freely than anyone. And without freedom, radical innovation remains episodic.

Ultimately, China stands before a crossroads that Jin does not articulate clearly enough: continue along the catch-up path, with guaranteed but increasingly marginal returns, or open itself to a model that allows ideas to emerge that the system cannot control. It is the tension between security and creativity, between order and imagination, between planning and intuition. And this tension is, today, the true fault line of China's future.

WHY POLITICAL CONTROL LIMITS THE VERY CREATIVITY JIN CELEBRATES

In Jin's vision, China has managed to reconcile two elements that often seem irreconcilable in Western societies: political stability and economic creativity. According to her, the Chinese system can guarantee order and coordination without suffocating the innovative energy of firms and researchers. It is a seductive thesis, especially for those eager to see "efficient" authoritarianism as a viable alternative to democratic complexity. But the thesis collapses the moment one observes how innovation actually behaves when it comes into contact with power. Political control—however rationalised or justified—inevitably constrains the very creativity Jin celebrates.

Creativity is not an orderly process. It does not arise from respect for rules but from their suspension; not from conformity but from deviation; not from obedience but from intellectual independence. It is a force that, by definition, escapes planning. No state can decide when or where a radical idea will emerge, or who will formulate it. The only necessary condition is that no one is afraid to think it. And this is precisely the condition that China's political system has made more difficult in recent years.

The first limit of political control is cognitive conformism.

In a system with a single ideological line—even when couched in broad terms such as "common prosperity," "national security," or "social stability"—researchers, entrepreneurs, and students learn to shape their ideas according to what is "acceptable." This is not only about direct censorship; it is the subtler, more pervasive phenomenon of self-censorship that reduces the capacity to formulate hypotheses that challenge the status quo. A researcher who knows that failure can cost a career will avoid risky experimentation; an entrepreneur who fears being perceived as a political threat will avoid products or services that redefine entire sectors. The effect is invisible but devastating: it limits ideas before they are even born.

The second limit is political uncertainty.

Despite its appearance of stability, the Chinese system is deeply unpredictable for innovators. Sudden political campaigns—against digital platforms, against private tutoring, against high-profile entrepreneurs—have made clear that no sector is entirely safe. But innovation requires time, long-term investment, and confidence in the continuity of rules. If today I can innovate but tomorrow I cannot be sure whether my innovation will be deemed "disruptive," I will not invest in the boldest line—I will invest in the safest one. And safe innovation is not radical innovation; it is maintenance of the present.

The third limit is the shrinking space for criticism.

Great scientific and technological revolutions often arise from critiques of dominant ideas. In China, openly criticising a directive, a political orientation, or an established model is difficult. Even in academia, radical criticism is tolerated only insofar as it has no political consequences. Yet innovation is born of contestation—conceptual, methodological, cultural. When this energy is channelled or neutralised, what remains is linear, incremental innovation but never destabilising breakthroughs. China excels at optimising what already exists; it struggles to invent what no one had anticipated.

The fourth limit is the absence of protected failure.

In the West, radical innovations emerged from repeated failures: laboratories burning through funds, startups collapsing, ideas that did not work. Innovation culture thrives on failed attempts. But a political system that interprets failure as inefficiency—or fears that failure could breed instability—tends to punish risk-takers. China does not lack individual courage; it lacks institutions that protect those who take risks and fail. Without failure, innovation cannot breathe.

The fifth limit is the centralisation of imagination.

When the state decides which sectors are strategic, which technologies must be developed, which priorities must guide research, it inevitably narrows the space for the unexpected. The issue is not planning itself—every state plans. The issue is the absence of alternatives: if all intellectual energy focuses only on state-funded sectors, everything at the margins is deemed irrelevant. Yet radical innovation often emerges from the margins, from grey zones, from fields not yet deemed "strategic." Chinese planning produces excellence where it looks; but radical innovation emerges where no one is looking.

Lastly, there is a deeper, philosophical limit: creativity requires inner space—space to doubt, to dissent, to waste time, to err, to be unobserved. A society in which every utterance is potentially political, in which every success can become an object of suspicion, in which every form of expression must be calibrated, does not offer such space. Creativity shrinks, disciplines itself, normalises itself. It survives, but it does not erupt.

Jin admires China's applied power—its industrial speed, its capacity to organise resources. But she confuses this energy with creative freedom. As long as China remains a system where political control defines the boundaries of what can be thought, innovation will never be fully radical. It may be brilliant, efficient, competitive, even surprising—but it will not be the forge of rupture Jin imagines.

The truth is simple: China excels at building the future it already knows; but radical innovation requires imagining the future it does not yet know. And in a system that fears creative disorder, that is the hardest point to reach.

The Economics of Control: Surveillance, Data, and Digital Authoritarianism

SOCIAL CREDIT, BIG DATA, ALGORITHMIC GOVERNANCE

When Jin speaks of China's modernity, she tends to emphasise the state's ability to use data to coordinate, monitor, and optimise economic functioning. It is a reassuring image: a country that harnesses digital technologies to govern more effectively, correct inefficiencies, and allocate resources more rationally. But this image, elegant as it is, fails to grasp the core of China's digital transformation. China has not merely digitalised its governance; it has politicised technology, turning it into an extension of state control. Surveillance, social credit, big data, and behavioural algorithms are not neutral instruments of modernisation; they are integral to a system that seeks to replace social trust with the technical management of behaviour.

The *first pillar* is social credit. In the West, it is often misunderstood as a single centralised system assigning every citizen a fixed score. In reality, it is a fragmented, complex ecosystem of public and private platforms, local registries, and sector-specific regulations. But the essential function is clear: to translate social reputation and civic behaviour into a record that can be evaluated—and potentially sanctioned. It is moral engineering in digital form. A citizen who fails to pay a fine can be restricted from buying train tickets; a business owner who violates regulations may be labelled "untrustworthy"; someone who criticises public figures may face service limitations. These mechanisms are not mere administrative simplifications: they create a culture of self-monitoring, prudence, and anticipatory conformity. When every gesture may leave a trace, social spontaneity shrinks.

The *second pillar* is the massive use of big data. China collects information on a scale unimaginable in any advanced democracy: facial-recognition cameras, urban sensors, electronic health records, platform data, financial movements, social-media interactions—everything can be aggregated. And aggregation is not passive. The state does not simply observe: it analyses, classifies, predicts. Algorithmic governance is often presented as a tool for efficiency—preventing fraud, monitoring epidemics, optimising traffic—but its true purpose is political: to create a perpetual window into collective behaviour. A population under constant observation is not only easier to control; it is more predictable, and therefore governable according to logics that are not publicly negotiated.

The *third pillar* is algorithmic governance itself: the use of automated systems to guide—and sometimes decide—administrative and judicial matters. Algorithms classify firms by "trustworthiness," detect fiscal anomalies, and flag behaviours deemed risky for stability. This is not science fiction; it is already reality in many provinces. The promise is to eliminate human arbitrariness, corruption, and administrative slowness; the far more concrete risk is the creation of an impersonal, uncontestable authority in which political decisions are masked as technical neutrality. Such a system does not repress through force; it represses through probability. It does not punish explicit acts; it punishes patterns. And it does so in ways the citizen can barely understand.

The impact on society is profound. Permanent surveillance produces self-discipline: I restrain myself not because I fear punishment, but because I fear error. Psychologically, the distinction is crucial. Public life becomes a space of caution, calculation, and reputational self-protection. Social and cultural creativity flatten, because spontaneous expression risks colliding with algorithmic logics that no one fully knows. It is a new kind of authoritarianism: not visible, hierarchical, and repressive, but predictive, preventive, and distributed.

Jin sees in this digital ecosystem a competitive advantage: a state that knows what is happening in real time can intervene more quickly, coordinate better, prevent crises. But she does not consider the other side of the coin: the same mechanism creates a society that is less free, less daring, less willing to take risks.

Social and economic innovation requires pockets of unpredictability, shadows, unmonitored spaces where ideas can emerge that break the rules before rewriting them. A system of total surveillance compresses these spaces until they become marginal.

There is also a subtler but decisive limit: *the concentration of informational power*. Whoever controls data controls the narrative. And whoever controls the narrative controls the imaginable future. Algorithmic governance does not merely classify; it produces reality through visibility, selection, and omission. When the state becomes the arbiter of data, it can decide which problems are real and which are not, which phenomena merit attention and which must be obscured, which signals deserve interpretation and which must be ignored. Society loses the ability to see itself, describe itself, and criticise itself. Informational power is not just an instrument: it is political capital.

Ultimately, the economics of control is not a deviation from the Chinese model; it is its internal evolution—functional, efficient, technologically sophisticated, but profoundly restrictive. Jin sees in it a mark of modernity; what her analysis lacks is the recognition that control, once it becomes infrastructure, cannot coexist harmoniously with the diffuse creativity she attributes to China. Control produces order, but innovation demands disorder. And without disorder, China risks becoming a technologically advanced yet intellectually enclosed country: an algorithmic power unable to truly imagine the new.

EFFICIENCY OR SERVITUDE? THE QUESTION JIN AVOIDS

At this point in her narrative, Jin performs an intellectual move that appears convincing but, on closer inspection, reveals a deep fracture: she conflates efficiency with consent, order with freedom, stability with individual sovereignty. In her model, digital control appears as a natural extension of China's administrative efficiency — a modern, rational, even elegant way of overcoming Western bureaucratic rigidity. The automation of governance becomes a sign of systemic superiority. Surveillance, when mentioned at all, appears as a minimal sacrifice in exchange for a society that "works." It is a narrative that reassures the economist, because it makes optimisation coincide with progress.

But the question Jin avoids is precisely this: the line between efficiency and servitude is exceedingly thin. And in a system where technologies of control are not tools but the architecture of power itself, that line risks disappearing.

In any complex society, power wants to know. But what distinguishes a democracy from an authoritarian regime is not the quantity of data collected; it is the direction of transparency. In a democracy, the state is transparent to its citizens; in a surveillance regime, the citizens are transparent to the state. Jin celebrates China's ability to "see" what happens within the country, but never asks who is allowed to see the state. The result is a model in which informational asymmetry becomes political asymmetry: the citizen is observable, the state is opaque. And it is precisely in this opacity that efficiency morphs into servitude.

Jin's argument assumes that control is exercised benevolently, with economic purpose and utilitarian rationality. But power is never so linear. Tools created to "optimise" can be used to discipline; tools devised to monitor financial risk can be used to monitor political risk; tools designed to track commercial behaviour can be used to track dissent. The history of technology shows that no infrastructure of control ever remains confined to its original purpose. Once mastery over data is established, efficiency becomes the language through which servitude justifies itself.

Jin's blind spot is the belief that a system that functions well is automatically a legitimate system. But efficiency is not a moral criterion. A society can be extremely efficient at repression, standardisation, and the neutralisation of dissent. The question is not whether algorithmic governance increases efficiency. The question is who defines what is efficient, for whom, against whom, and with what possibility of contestation. The Chinese citizen does not live in a system where he can interrogate power; he lives in a system where power can interrogate him at any moment. And this is not a technical detail: it is the core of modern servitude.

There is a second, even more delicate question: the transformation of obedience into automatism. Digital surveillance does not simply forbid behaviours; it prevents them. It does not punish only acts; it punishes inclinations. It does not correct mistakes; it anticipates them. This is a form of servitude without drama, without conflict, without visible violence — a servitude interiorised through incentives, scores, conditional access, algorithmic reputations. A servitude that turns individuals into nodes in a behavioural computation system. It is the masterpiece of twenty-first-century authoritarianism: power that does not impose itself, but insinuates itself; that does not repress, but optimises.

Jin imagines that such a system can foster trust, because it reduces uncertainty and guarantees order. But trust does not emerge from the predictability of behaviour; it emerges from the ability to speak without fear, to dissent without disappearing, to know that authority is not omniscient. Without this dimension, trust is not a sentiment: it is a form of resignation. This is what Jin fails to articulate: she confuses compliance with cohesion, silence with consent.

Finally, there is a philosophical point that her narrative entirely elides: efficiency is an instrumental value, not a foundational one. A society does not exist to be efficient; it exists to be just, free, fertile with possibilities. Efficiency can maximise output, but it cannot replace dignity. It can improve logistics, but it cannot generate autonomy. It can govern better, but it cannot justify a power that admits no limits.

This is the question Jin avoids: if efficiency becomes the supreme criterion, then any form of servitude can be justified as optimisation. But a society that confuses docility with order, and predictability with peace, is not a more modern society; it is a more domesticated one. China is not destined for this trajectory, but the infrastructures it is building make the choice between efficiency and freedom increasingly irreversible.

And if the Chinese model is to be assessed seriously, one must say it without ambiguity: an efficient power can be far more dangerous than an inefficient one. For it makes servitude functional. And functional servitude is the hardest kind to recognise — and the easiest to accept.

THE ECONOMIC COST OF FEAR

Jin celebrates order as a productive force: a disciplined society, in her view, is one that can concentrate resources, avoid conflict, act swiftly, correct imbalances before they escalate. But what her analysis omits is the reverse side of this order: fear. Not the spectacular fear of visible repression — which modern China uses relatively sparingly — but a diffuse, molecular, everyday fear. The fear that leads one to choose the safest path, to avoid the idea that is too new, the word that is too free, the criticism that is too explicit. It is a fear that does not paralyse the system but cools it; that does not halt growth but limits its depth; that does not stop innovation but makes it timid, conservative, predictable.

This fear has an economic cost — precise, measurable, cumulative. And it is a cost Jin does not account for.

The first cost is the slowing of private initiative. In a context where political lines can shift suddenly, where entire sectors can be struck by regulatory campaigns, where successful entrepreneurial figures can be removed from public life without explanation, the appetite for risk diminishes. Firms invest less in non-guaranteed innovations, prefer to align with state priorities, avoid expanding into directions that might be interpreted as challenges to power. What Jin calls "coordination," in the lived experience of entrepreneurs, is a mixture of caution and self-restraint. And when entrepreneurs become fearful, the market contracts.

The second cost is the impoverishment of the creative ecosystem. Art, culture, the humanities, intellectual debate are not marginal sectors: they are the spaces where a society learns to think differently. When these spaces are normalised, economic creativity weakens. Innovative societies do not emerge from laboratories alone; they emerge in cities where cultural experimentation is possible. But a society that fears expressing itself is a society that creates less, imagines less, dares less. The economic potential of a nation also depends on its imaginative capacity — and imagination does not flourish in fear.

The third cost is the rigidity of human capital. A population that fears failure does not make bold choices. It prefers stable jobs to risky ventures, linear paths to creative ones, the known to the uncertain. This is not merely a cultural limitation: it is an economic one. The most dynamic economies are those in which young people can afford to fail, to change course, to reinvent themselves. But in a system that rewards conformity and punishes deviation, human capital adapts by becoming conservative. It becomes a human capital that executes, not invents.

The fourth cost is the flight of the best talent. Many highly qualified young Chinese, especially in scientific and technological fields, seek opportunities abroad. Not for lack of patriotism, but for lack of space. They want to live in environments where freedom is experienced rather than regulated; where professional growth does not depend on political alignment; where an idea can be pursued without wondering whether it violates an invisible boundary. China invests enormously in education, but risks losing part of its most valuable human capital not for economic reasons but for psychological and cultural ones. It is a form of brain drain less visible than in the 1990s, but far more dangerous.

The fifth cost is the institutionalisation of uncertainty. Paradoxically, a system that aims at total control produces continuous uncertainty: no one knows precisely where the limits lie, which behaviours will be tolerated, which innovations will be deemed dangerous, which sectors will be targeted by the next political campaign. This uncertainty is not an accident: it is a structural effect of control. And when uncertainty becomes a regime, investments shrink, long-term projects weaken, productivity slows.

Finally, there is a deeper cost, harder to measure but more devastating: the cost of renunciation. Renunciation of honest speech, of criticism, of creative madness. Renunciation of the disorderly gesture that can open a new path. Renunciation of the possibility of imagining a future that has not already been authorised. Economies feed on what people dream; and when dreams must pass through the filter of caution, they become smaller.

Jin sees a confident country, ready to challenge the West with an alternative model. But a country that does not fully admit the freedom of its citizens is a country that limits its own economic strength. Control produces order, but fear produces mediocrity — and no economic system, however efficient, can prosper long on widespread mediocrity.

China possesses extraordinary power, but fear restrains it — invisibly, daily, cumulatively. It is the cost Jin does not calculate. It is the cost no statistic can show. It is the cost that, in the long run, separates societies that produce progress from those that merely imitate it.

PART III

CHINA AND THE WORLD: GEOPOLITICS IN THE TWENTY-FIRST CENTURY

The Economic War with the United States: Beyond Hyperbole

TECHNOLOGY, SEMICONDUCTORS, SUPPLY CHAINS

When people speak of the "new Cold War" between China and the United States, the dominant rhetoric is often exaggerated: they evoke inevitable conflicts, total decoupling, opposing blocs as though the world were returning to 1950. Jin, though more measured, insists that the technological confrontation is primarily the result of American fear: America fears a China that innovates, grows, and competes. But this interpretation fails to grasp the true nature of the competition and its deeper implications. The rivalry does not stem from psychological resentment; it stems from a material fact: for the first time in history, an authoritarian power is capable of competing with the United States in frontier technological sectors. This is unprecedented geopolitically — and even more unprecedented ideologically.

The heart of the competition is not trade, but technology. Semiconductors, in particular, are not simply an industrial sector: they are the infrastructure of contemporary power. Controlling the ability to produce advanced chips means controlling artificial intelligence, automation, aerospace, cybersecurity, cryptography, and military robotics. The American strategy of limiting China's access to the most advanced technologies (extreme ultraviolet lithography, 5 nm chips and below, key design components) is therefore not an act of "hostility" in the emotional sense: it is a measure of strategic containment directed at a competitor capable of reshaping the global balance.

China, for its part, understands what is at stake. And this is where Jin's narrative becomes more nuanced — but also more naïve. Jin argues that American restrictions, far from slowing China, have made it more determined and more autonomous, forcing massive domestic investment in research, design, and manufacturing. This is true: in some areas, China's response has been rapid and impressive. But Jin fails to consider the structural limit: technological catch-up in semiconductors does not function like catch-up in manufacturing. Here, it is not enough to invest capital or mobilize engineers: what is needed is a global ecosystem, made of distributed knowledge, international exchange, and highly specialized supply chains. And this ecosystem — no matter how much China may try to replicate it — currently depends on technologies and expertise held firmly by the United States, Japan, the Netherlands, South Korea, and Taiwan.

The case of Taiwan is emblematic. Jin tends to present the Taiwan–China interdependence as mutually beneficial: China depends on chips produced on the island; the island depends on the Chinese market and manufacturing. But this interdependence is asymmetrical: China cannot autonomously produce advanced chips, while Taiwan can sell most of its output elsewhere. The dependency is not symmetrical; it is political. And this is one of the reasons why the Taiwan question remains central to China's strategy.

Jin also underestimates the significance of global supply chains. For thirty years China has been the heart of world manufacturing because it offered what no other country offered: abundant labor, highly efficient logistics, limitless capacity for expansion and adaptation. But with rising costs, demographic contraction, political pressure, and geopolitical tensions, many companies are diversifying — not out of hostility to China, but to reduce risk. Vietnam, India, Mexico, and Indonesia are attracting parts of the manufacturing that once would have gone automatically to China. This is not "isolating" China: it is a rebalancing of the global system. But it is a rebalancing that reveals something fundamental: the world no longer sees China as a neutral partner, but as a political actor capable of influencing global economic stability in unpredictable ways.

It is important to understand that total decoupling is unrealistic — for the West and for China alike. The complexity of supply chains, mutual dependence in critical sectors, and the enormous cost of a clean break make such a scenario borderline science fiction. What is happening is not decoupling, but de-risking: a gradual reduction of structural vulnerability. And it is precisely this transition that Jin does not address with sufficient depth. The world is not separating from China; it is ceasing to treat China as an indispensable pivot of the global production system.

China, meanwhile, does not face an easy choice. To compete with the United States it must innovate; but to innovate it must open up, collaborate, interact with international networks that partly fear it. Its technological strength is real, but its vulnerability is equally real: Chinese innovation lives within a deeply interconnected economy that political power attempts to control. This tension is one Jin underestimates, because she believes in a harmonious model in which politics and economics reinforce one another. The technological war shows the opposite: when politics overreaches in its control, the economy loses oxygen.

In short, the competition between the United States and China is not a cultural war or a psychological conflict: it is the first battle over the architecture of twenty-first-century technology. The winner will not be the one who imitates best, nor the one who invests the most, but the one who can build the most fertile, open, and flexible ecosystem. And here, China has extraordinary strengths — but also deep vulnerabilities that Jin prefers not to confront.

THE POSSIBLE DECOUPLING, THE IMPOSSIBLE ONE, AND THE ONE THAT HAS ALREADY HAPPENED

The word *decoupling* is often used as though it described a clean break — a dramatic, sudden event. Jin treats it as an exaggerated threat, a kind of specter waved by the West to justify protectionist measures. But this view ignores the real nature of the phenomenon: decoupling is not a leap, but a process; not a wall, but a set of fault lines opening simultaneously in different directions. To understand what is happening, we must distinguish among three levels: what can be separated, what cannot be separated under any circumstance, and what has already separated without anyone fully noticing.

The first level concerns the most advanced and most sensitive sectors of global competition. Here, decoupling is not only possible: it is already underway. Next-generation semiconductors, extreme ultraviolet lithography, GPUs designed for artificial intelligence, and dual-use technologies tied to national security are now at the center of a technical separation that no diplomatic cooperation can undo. The United States has built barriers isolating China from access to frontier technologies. China is responding with massive domestic investment in research and production. The result is not a total wall, but a bifurcation of technological trajectories: two systems developing in parallel, no longer symmetrically. This is the *possible* decoupling: the one that affects areas where interdependence is not vital and where the geopolitical stakes are too high to be shared.

The second level concerns everything from which separation is impossible. Global manufacturing, despite diversification efforts, remains anchored to China for structural reasons: logistics, infrastructure, industrial know-how, integrated supply chains, and the capacity to scale at extraordinary speed. Neither the United States nor Europe nor Southeast Asia can replace China's productive ecosystem in the short term. The same holds for strategic raw materials and for the technologies required for the energy transition: rare-earth refining, battery production, photovoltaic components. The dependence is mutual, but above all it is irreducible. And then there is consumption: China is too large, too wealthy, too interconnected a market for Western multinationals to forgo without inflicting structural damage on themselves. This is the *impossible* decoupling: the one that belongs to the material physiology of the world.

The third level is the most important — and paradoxically the one Jin fails to address: the *invisible* decoupling, the one that does not appear in trade data but that shapes every strategic decision. It is the decoupling of trust. In recent years, the assumption that China and the West share a common destiny or systemic compatibility has eroded. Governments, firms, universities, and financial institutions have begun to behave as though cooperation were fragile, conditional, and reversible. Bilateral investment has fallen to levels last seen twenty years ago; scientific collaborations have been scaled back; cybersecurity has become a matter of national survival; the very idea of China as a neutral partner has vanished. This decoupling has already happened, and it is deeply rooted: once two systems stop trusting each other, no economic interdependence can repair the fracture.

This is where Jin's reading shows its limits. She treats decoupling as an attempt by the West to slow China down, not as the result of a growing incompatibility between political models and technological architectures. She ignores that the competition does not arise from American emotion but from an objective fact: a digital authoritarian system is emerging as a global technological power. And she underestimates the significance of a world that, while continuing to trade with China, has stopped perceiving it as a reliable partner.

The possible decoupling will continue to grow; the impossible one will continue to bind us; the one already accomplished will shape the century. And it is this last one — not the others — that defines the new geopolitics: the world has not decoupled from China in goods, but it has decoupled from China in trust. In the long run, that separation weighs more than any tariff or embargo.

JIN'S INTERPRETATION: WHERE SHE IS TOO OPTIMISTIC, AND WHERE SHE IS TOO CAUTIOUS

The strength of Jin's book lies in her ability to restore to China a complexity often missing from Western narratives: not a menacing giant, not a monolithic empire, but a country in transformation, full of contradictions, energies, and ambitions.

Precisely for this reason, however, her omissions matter more. Her analysis is brilliant, but not neutral: she leans in certain directions and retreats from others. Her vision is optimistic where it should be more severe, and cautious where it should be clearer. This imbalance reveals not so much a lack of expertise as a structural limit of her intellectual project: describing China from within without truly coming into conflict with its political system.

The first instance of excessive optimism concerns the technological model. Jin sees China as a power that has already moved beyond the imitative phase and is entering a stage of autonomous innovation. She correctly notes the progress, the investments, the scientific energy, but ignores the contradictions stemming from the incompatibility between political control and radical creativity. She is too optimistic when she treats algorithmic governance as a simple tool of efficiency; too optimistic when she assumes China can quickly close the gap in semiconductors; too optimistic when she reads China's response to U.S. restrictions as an inevitable acceleration. She does not see that some limits are not technical but systemic: they cannot be overcome by building more laboratories, but by changing the political environment in which those laboratories operate.

The second excess of optimism concerns social resilience. Jin interprets the Chinese ability to endure hardship as evidence of collective strength, without asking how this resilience transforms once the promise of upward mobility — the psychological engine of China's miracle — begins to fade. She is too optimistic when she assumes new generations will accept sacrifices similar to those of previous ones; too optimistic when she interprets disciplined behavior as a sign of cohesion rather than caution; too optimistic when she treats society as a stable actor and not as a subject undergoing rapid demographic and psychological erosion.

The third locus of excessive optimism is the State's ability to correct its own mistakes. Jin highlights the adaptability of the Chinese political system, its skill in adjusting economic strategies, controlling capital allocation, directing industrial transformation. But she does not sufficiently consider the growing institutional rigidity of recent years. The era of experimental reforms is long over; the apparatus is more centralized, more suspicious, more risk-averse. Jin views China as if it were still the China of the 2000s: a fluid, pragmatic policy laboratory. Today's China is a system far less permeable and far more ideological.

Where Jin is too cautious — and this caution is as consequential as her optimism — is in describing the political limits of the model. Her language becomes opaque whenever she ought to discuss the concentration of power, the absence of distinction between State and Party, the repression of dissent, digital surveillance, and the pervasive fear within the private sector. She is too cautious when she speaks of governance and remains silent about the nature of the regime; too cautious when she describes political security as a mere condition of stability; too cautious when she avoids confronting the Taiwan question as one of self-determination and treats it only as a geopolitical variable.

She is also cautious when assessing China's structural slowdown. She acknowledges the risks of debt, the real-estate crisis, and demography, but she consistently presents them as manageable challenges. It is an understandable reading for someone writing from within the system, but it risks trivializing the magnitude of an epochal shift: China is no longer a country on automatic growth; it is a country that must reinvent a model that cannot function as before.

Finally, Jin is cautious where she should be more decisive in distinguishing what works because it is effective from what works because it is imposed. This distinction — the key to understanding contemporary China — never appears with clarity in her book.

Jin's interpretation is valuable because it restores complexity, but incomplete because it avoids the most uncomfortable part: the structural tension between power and creativity, between growth and control, between global ambitions and internal limits. She is too optimistic about technological autonomy, too cautious about the political nature of the system, too confident in social resilience, too timid in acknowledging that efficiency can become servitude.

Her account illuminates much, but leaves in shadow what will truly determine China's future. And it is precisely for this reason that it must be supplemented, corrected, and, where necessary, contradicted.

Europe Between Naivety and Dependence

EUROPE BETWEEN NAIVETY AND DEPENDENCE

Europe has always viewed China through a filter that makes it simultaneously more fascinating and less comprehensible. The United States sees China as a strategic rival, a direct competitor in defining the global order, a systemic adversary undermining its leadership. This clarity comes from direct confrontation: two technological empires, two political models, two opposing visions of globalization.

Europe, by contrast, does not perceive itself as a comparable global power; and precisely for this reason it tends to interpret China not as a structural threat but as a managerial challenge, a difficult partner, a commercial opportunity to be balanced with a few moral obligations. This is the root of a myopia that Jin, curiously, never addresses: Europe does not understand China because it does not understand itself.

The first European mistake is excessive economic reductionism. Europe has convinced itself that China is above all an economic actor — a gigantic market, the world's factory. It focuses on tariffs, quotas, direct investment, technological transfers, but misses the essential point: for China, the economy is not an end, but a political means. The Party does not seek wealth; it seeks power, cohesion, legitimacy. Europe continues to reason as if China were a commercial competitor with similar categories of interest, ignoring that every Chinese decision passes through a political system with no equivalent on the continent.

The second mistake is naïve faith in normative soft power. Europe has always believed that its model — rule of law, multilateralism, regulation, social democracy — possesses a natural force of attraction. It assumes that, over time, China will converge toward similar standards: more market, more transparency, more rights, more cooperation. This belief in "convergence" has been Europe's greatest illusion. China has never wanted to converge; it has wanted to interact on its own terms. And today, far from being transformed by Europe, it is China that is transforming Europe, forcing it to rethink its strategic innocence.

The third European mistake is internal fragmentation. The United States treats China as a unified dossier; Europe treats it as a patchwork of national interests: Germany looks at automotive exports, Italy at infrastructure investments, France at strategic autonomy, Eastern Europe at the American presence.

Each country reads China through its own immediate commercial advantage, not through a common strategy. The result is paradoxical: Europe, which would most need a unified policy to deal with such a concentrated power, instead presents itself as a mosaic of negotiable vulnerabilities.

The fourth mistake is the moral misunderstanding. Many European elites view China through ethical categories — human rights, civil liberties, minorities — without understanding that these categories, however crucial, are no longer sufficient to orient geopolitical strategy. China does not respond to moral suasion. It does not engage with what it does not respect. And when Europe speaks the language of rights without translating it into real leverage, China listens politely and then ignores it. It is a dialogue between a normative code and a power code: incompatible.

The fifth mistake is the underestimation of digital authoritarianism. The United States immediately understood that the Huawei question was not commercial but political: it concerned the possibility that a global infrastructure could be controlled by an authoritarian regime. Europe, by contrast, oscillated for years between openness and fear, as if the problem were purely technological. Chinese digital authoritarianism has not been understood in its deeper nature: a new, exportable, adaptable, and seductive model of governance for many non-democratic countries. Europe, bound to an outdated conception of power, struggles to see the challenge for what it is: systemic.

Finally, Europe understands China worse than the U.S. because it no longer has a living memory of authoritarianism. Too many decades of peace and prosperity have dulled its ability to recognize an illiberal regime for what it is. Where the U.S. sees an adversary, Europe sees a difficult partner. Where the U.S. sees a battle over the standards of the twenty-first century, Europe sees commercial competition. Where the U.S. sees a strategic risk, Europe sees a moral dilemma. It is a form of blindness — unintentional, but profound.

Jin's interpretation does not correct this blindness; it reinforces it. She presents a China that is rational, moderate, essentially economic; a China that does not threaten, does not export models, does not seek to redefine the world's rules. It is a reassuring narrative for a continent that has stopped thinking of itself as a power and that would prefer not to choose.

But China will force Europe to choose regardless — between autonomy and dependence, between naivety and realism, between a worldview that defends itself and one that allows itself to be reshaped. And as long as Europe continues to interpret China through economic and moral categories rather than geopolitical ones, it will continue to understand it worse than the United States. Not because it is less intelligent, but because it is less accustomed — and less willing — to look power in the eye.

THE TRAP OF "ASYMMETRIC COOPERATION"

If there is one concept that best summarizes Europe's approach to China over the past twenty years, it is precisely this: asymmetric cooperation. It is a relationship in which both sides speak of cooperation, but one cooperates in a conditional and strategic way, while the other cooperates in an open and naïve one. In her narrative, Jin describes China as a partner operating according to pragmatic, mutually beneficial logics. But what she does not say is that Chinese cooperation is always structured to produce asymmetry: technological, informational, regulatory, diplomatic. Europe, which confuses cooperation with symmetry, falls straight into the trap.

China cooperates only where cooperation strengthens its strategic margin. Europe cooperates because it believes cooperation is a value in itself. The difference is not cultural: it is geopolitical.

The first point of the trap is *asymmetry of access*. European companies in China must operate within rigidly defined political, sectoral, and legal limits. Chinese companies in Europe, by contrast, have enjoyed — or enjoyed until recently — almost unlimited access: acquisitions, investments, installation of critical infrastructure, participation in strategic sectors. Europe opened doors that China kept half-shut. Jin speaks of "cultural barriers" or "adjustment periods," but avoids the essential point: symmetry is not part of the Chinese model.

The second point is *technological asymmetry*. For years, Europe shared technologies, industrial standards, know-how, often without demanding equivalent guarantees. China absorbed this knowledge and integrated it into a controlled ecosystem from which Europe has been progressively excluded. The European belief that industrial cooperation is always win–win ignores a simple fact: China does not cooperate to enrich the other side; it cooperates to accelerate itself.

The third point is *informational asymmetry*. China studies Europe in depth: its institutions, regulations, public opinion, political parties, social vulnerabilities. Europe, instead, has only a fragmented, superficial understanding of China, often mediated through inadequate Western categories. Diplomatic cooperation works only if both sides understand each other's codes; but China studies Europe, while Europe assumes it understands China without truly studying it. It is cooperation that produces opacity on one side and transparency on the other.

The fourth point is *geopolitical asymmetry*. For China every commercial agreement, every technological partnership, every economic initiative is embedded in a strategy of power. Europe, too often, evaluates these agreements in terms of growth, exports, sector-specific opportunities. Europe negotiates contracts; China negotiates positions. Europe looks at the next legislature; China looks at the next thirty years. This divergence of horizons creates a form of cooperation that always advantages the party capable of thinking in the long term.

The fifth point is *narrative asymmetry*. China controls its own image with millimetric precision: what may be said, what may be shown, what must be interpreted. Europe, by contrast, presents itself with radical transparency, where opinions, internal debates, and public conflicts become immediately visible to the other side. China sees Europe from the inside; Europe sees China through the official showcase. This is not cooperation: it is imbalance.

This trap appears in emblematic form in the Belt and Road Initiative. European countries signed memoranda convinced it was an infrastructure project; China used it to build strategic footholds, diplomatic influence, economic dependencies. What for Europe was an act of cooperation, for China was an act of positioning. Both sides believed they were acting within the same framework, but their mental maps were entirely different.

Jin, in her book, mentions this asymmetry but does not develop it. She describes it as a cultural misunderstanding, a difference of priorities, a problem solvable through more dialogue. But it is not a problem of dialogue: it is a structural one. Chinese cooperation never seeks symmetry; it seeks management of advantage. Europe keeps falling into the trap because it has not yet accepted that symmetry, for China, is not a principle: it is a strategic mistake.

To escape this trap, Europe must make a choice that is simple in theory but difficult in practice: stop cooperating as a value, and start cooperating as a strategy. Not closing off, but understanding that openness cannot be unilateral; not distrusting everything, but distrusting intelligently; not abandoning dialogue, but balancing it with the ability to negotiate as an equal.

As long as Europe continues to believe that "cooperation" automatically means "equilibrium," it will continue to be surprised by a China playing a different game, with different rules, on a chessboard Europe has not yet learned to see.

HOW EUROPE CAN AVOID BECOMING A HUNTING GROUND

Europe is today, in the eyes of China (and not only China), an open, permeable, fragmented, vulnerable territory: a place where external interests can infiltrate, steer decisions, acquire strategic assets, influence public opinion, and exploit internal rivalries among Member States. This is not a moral judgment: it is a geopolitical observation. When a unified, centralized, strategically coherent power interacts with a disunited, norm-driven continent obsessed with internal consensus, the outcome is almost inevitable: Europe becomes a hunting ground. Not because it is economically weak, but because it is politically weak.

To avoid this condition — which is not yet irreversible, but will become so if nothing changes — Europe must confront three uncomfortable truths.

The first: no economic openness has value without the ability to defend it.

Europe opened its markets believing that reciprocity would be automatic, that transparency would produce transparency, that trust would generate trust. But openness is sustainable only when one also has the strength to select, negotiate, block, and impose rules. As long as Europe does not develop genuinely integrated investment-screening tools, common standards for critical infrastructure, and shared criteria for evaluating the entry of external actors into sensitive sectors, every European country will remain free to become the weak point of the entire continent. China has skillfully exploited these divisions: investing where it was easiest, acquiring infrastructure where governments were most compliant, building political ties where vulnerability was highest. To avoid being hunted, Europe must learn to close selectively, to choose, to say no with the same confidence with which it has always said yes.

The second truth: internal competition is geopolitical suicide.

Germany thinks about cars, France about strategic sovereignty, Italy about infrastructure, Eastern Europe about American protection. This plurality is not a strength: it is the perfect incentive for anyone seeking to penetrate the continent by dividing its fronts. As long as Europe fails to speak with one voice, China will continue dealing with each country separately, offering bilateral deals, targeted investments, customized commercial advantages. Europe can avoid becoming a hunting ground only if it stops presenting itself as a savannah full of isolated animals and begins to behave like an ecosystem. This does not mean erasing differences, but preventing them from being exploited against it. It means introducing a simple principle: no European country negotiates with China alone on strategic matters. Anyone accepting Chinese investments in ports, energy grids, telecommunications, or artificial intelligence must do so within a European framework. Without this discipline, Europe will keep selling pieces of its own future in exchange for short-term opportunities.

The third truth: there is no autonomy without technological power.

Europe today depends on China in key sectors: batteries, solar panels, rare-earth processing, electronic components. This dependency is not only the result of poor industrial policy, but of a lack of strategic vision: Europe assumed the world would remain a place of benign interdependence, where the most efficient produces and the others buy. China believed exactly the opposite: that technological dominance is the condition of sovereignty. If Europe wants to stop being a hunting ground, it must build its own strategic supply chains. Not all of them — that would be impossible — but some. Chips, renewable energy, artificial intelligence, biotechnology: without autonomous productive capacity in at least part of these sectors, Europe will always be forced to depend on the outside, and those who depend do not negotiate — they endure.

To these three truths a fourth, even more uncomfortable, must be added:

Europe must stop deluding itself that China can be transformed through trade.

This myth has guided twenty years of EU–China relations. It is a dead myth. China will not converge toward the European model; it will not adopt European-style multilateralism; it will not internalize European normative frameworks; it will not accept an international system shaped by the EU. Europe must finally treat China for what it is: an intelligent authoritarian power, aggressive when necessary, skilled in negotiation, masterful in using interdependence as an instrument of power. This is not a moral judgment: it is a fact.

And yet Europe should not turn itself into a hostile fortress or a paranoid power. The point is not to close — it is to choose.

Choose where to cooperate, where to compete, where to protect itself.

Choose which sectors to open, which to shield, which to share.

Choose how to strengthen itself internally so it cannot be manipulated externally.

Europe becomes a hunting ground when it is predictable, fragmented, eager to attract investment at any cost. It can stop being one only if it becomes what it has forgotten to be: a power. Not an aggressive power, but a conscious one. A power that does not seek to dominate, but refuses to be dominated. A power that cooperates as an equal, not as prey.

China does not respect weakness; it respects strength.

And as long as Europe does not show strength — in its unity, in its technology, in its ability to say “no” — it will remain exactly what China sees today: a place full of opportunities, and therefore a perfect territory for those who know how to hunt.

Belt and Road and the New Global Order

LOANS, PORTS, INFRASTRUCTURE, DEBT DIPLOMACY

Loans, ports, infrastructure, debt diplomacy

The Belt and Road Initiative (BRI) is often presented — including by Jin — as a vast infrastructure project: bridges, railways, highways, ports, special economic zones, energy corridors. It is a tidy, almost engineering-like narrative that supports a reassuring idea: China builds, China connects, China invests in the Global South, China fills the "infrastructure gap" left by the West. There is some truth in this vision, but it omits what matters most. The BRI is not an economic plan: it is a strategy for ordering the world. It is not an industrial project: it is a political — indeed *geostructural* — project. Where the West saw markets, China sees corridors; where the West saw investment, China sees leverage; where the West saw cooperation, China sees positioning.

Chinese loans, the centerpiece of this architecture, are not equivalent to Western multilateral loans. The financial conditions — often opaque, bilaterally negotiated, with interest rates neither scandalous nor generous — are only part of the story. The defining feature of BRI loans is political collateralization: guarantees on ports, mines, infrastructure, exploitation rights, long-term concessions, confidentiality clauses that prevent debtor governments from disclosing agreement terms. China does not simply lend money: it lends money in exchange for positions. And positions, today, matter more than capital.

Ports are the most obvious example. Chinese acquisitions or concessions in Sri Lanka, Pakistan, Greece, Djibouti, Egypt, Italy (before the memorandum was scaled back), Israel, Tanzania outline a logistical map that no power has ever built so quickly. This is not colonialism: it is geoeconomics with Chinese characteristics. Logistics is power: the power to influence maritime routes, to guarantee commercial privileges, to create asymmetric dependencies. A port is never "just a port": it is an access point, an observation post, a data archive, an infrastructure that shapes political relations far beyond what appears in diplomatic communiqués.

The third pillar of the BRI is domestic infrastructure in partner countries: railways, highways, dams, power plants. These projects are often celebrated as contributions to Global South development — and in part, they are. But they are not designed to strengthen local economies; they are designed to connect the partner country to China. The logic is that of the corridor: linking extractive zones with controlled ports, tying production areas to trade flows toward Asia, creating a network of material dependencies that make integration with China more convenient than diversification. BRI infrastructures are arteries: they pump value toward the center of the system, not toward the periphery.

Then there is debt diplomacy — the most contested and most misunderstood aspect of the BRI. It is not — as some Western narratives claim — a deliberate plan to indebt countries and then seize their infrastructure. It is something subtler and more effective: a mechanism through which China becomes indispensable. When an indebted country cannot repay, China does not necessarily demand ownership of the project: it asks for privileged access, long-term contracts, strategic participation, diplomatic alignment. Debt becomes a language: there is no need to demand; one only needs to remind. And many governments, especially politically fragile ones, prefer alignment over renegotiation.

In this system, Jin sees above all the benefits for developing countries: infrastructure where none existed, investments the West no longer offered, a partner willing to do what the IMF would not. But this is only part of the picture. The other — the more decisive one — is that China uses the BRI to build a global network of functional dependencies, where trade is no longer exchange but leverage; where investment is no longer cooperation but constraint; where economic geography reshapes political geography.

It took the West years to understand that the BRI was not an infrastructure program but a form of alternative international order. An order in which China does not export ideology but method: centralization, negotiating opacity, bilateralism, informal conditionality, primacy of political ties over multilateral rules. It is an order that many countries find easier to navigate because it does not demand democratic reforms, impose environmental or social standards, or interfere in domestic affairs. In exchange, it asks for loyalty. A gradual, undeclared, but real loyalty.

The BRI does not aim to replace the West. It aims to make it irrelevant in contexts where an infrastructure can be worth more than a treaty. It is an order of low normative intensity and high material intensity. And it works because Europe and the United States abdicated this type of politics for years.

Jin sees the BRI as proof of China's ability to "create value where others do not see it." That is true. But she omits that the BRI does not only create value: it creates dependency, influence, asymmetry. It is not a development project: it is a world-making project. Those who analyze it with purely economic tools will never fully understand it. It is geopolitics in its purest form, disguised as civil engineering.

And this is why the BRI is essential for understanding contemporary China: because it reveals what Jin does not say openly. China does not simply want to grow; it wants to reorder the world according to its own logic. The BRI is its most sophisticated instrument. And to truly understand it, one must look not at the bridges, but at the power relations those bridges construct.

CHINESE STRATEGIC VISION VS. JIN'S TECHNICAL NARRATIVE

The deepest difference between what China does and what Jin describes is not a matter of facts but of levels of analysis. Jin views China through the lens of an economist: supply and demand, incentives, reforms, investment, growth, governance. Her attention is directed toward mechanisms, not intentions; toward internal dynamics, not the external architecture of power. It is a technical narrative — often brilliant — but inevitably partial. China, by contrast, thinks and acts as a historical power, not as an economic laboratory: its strategy is political, structural, temporal. It does not look at flows; it looks at forms. It does not look at today's balances; it looks at tomorrow's margins. It does not focus on what is happening now, but on what will be possible thirty years from now. This distance between Jin's technical level and China's strategic level is what generates the greatest interpretative distortions.

Jin's technical narrative tends to portray the Chinese system as a complex but rational machine, engaged in solving concrete problems: internal inequality, slowing growth, innovation, urbanization, the financial system, the technological challenge. Each issue is treated as an administrative problem: better incentives are needed, reforms must be calibrated, investment must be targeted, redistributive policies refined, a more stable balance between state and market restored. It is a vision that reduces power to its function as economic coordinator. But China does not use politics to distribute wealth: it uses wealth to redistribute power. This is a conceptual difference of scale that a purely economic reading cannot capture.

For the Chinese Party-State, strategy is not a set of reforms: it is a historical trajectory. Economic development has been, for forty years, the tool for consolidating domestic power and preparing the country for a more assertive role in the global order. It was never an end in itself. For this reason, China accepts slowdowns, inefficiencies, even structural mistakes, if they reinforce political cohesion or the country's international position. Jin's technical narrative assumes that growth is the central goal; China's strategic vision assumes that growth is only a phase — a phase used to build capacities: technological, military, logistical, industrial, cultural.

A striking example, as we have seen, is the Belt and Road: Jin describes it as economic policy, as win–win cooperation, as a response to the global infrastructure gap. In reality, for the Party, the BRI is a piece of a larger mosaic: an alternative world order based on bilateral dependencies, material corridors, financial influence, strategic autonomy. It is a project of power, not of development. The technical reading sees ports; the strategic reading sees positions.

The same applies to technology: Jin emphasizes scientific research, industrial innovation, R&D investment. But China invests in technology because technology is the new foundation of sovereignty. It does not study AI to improve productive efficiency, but to build an unprecedented regime of control. It does not develop semiconductors to compete in markets, but to reduce military and political vulnerability. It does not expand its global digital platforms to export products, but to export power architectures. Technology is not a sector: it is a geopolitical arena.

In Jin's narrative, the Party appears as a great regulator that corrects and directs; in reality, the Party is a strategic actor that steers the economy toward a political goal: shaping a world in which China is no longer constrained by Western institutions, global financial flows, market rules, or foreign technological limits. It is a project of geopolitical emancipation, disguised as economic modernization.

And again: the technical narrative sees Chinese "stability" as the ideal condition for development; the strategic vision sees stability as a necessary condition for preserving the Party's legitimacy. For Jin, stability is an economic virtue; for China, it is a political one. What is stable is what keeps the Party at the center. Everything else is variable.

Finally, there is a difference in the conception of time. Jin reasons in economic cycles: slowdown, recovery, reforms, investment. China reasons in epochs: the rise and fall of powers, the redistribution of global centers, the return of Asian influence, the correction of the post-1945 international order. The technical narrative is temporary; the strategic vision is teleological.

This divergence in perspective does not make Jin's book less useful; on the contrary, it makes it valuable as a diagnostic tool. But to truly understand China, one must complement it with what Jin does not say — or cannot say. One must restore politics to its central role, power to its logic, and the global order to its fragility. China does not think like an economist. It thinks like a civilization re-entering history with a precise project.

And between Jin's technical narrative and China's actual strategic vision runs the full distance that separates a brilliant description from a deep understanding.

THE GAME OF THE CENTURY: AFRICA

If there is one place in the world where the distance between Jin's technical narrative and China's strategic vision becomes visible as if under a microscope, it is Africa. Jin describes Africa as a space for economic cooperation: infrastructure investment, trade, opportunities for both sides. It is an elegant, even generous reading. But Africa, for China, is not a market: it is a historical frontier. It is the game of the century — the place where the global hierarchy of the first half of the twenty-first century will be determined.

The first essential point is that Africa matters not for what it is, but for what it will become. By 2050 it will host more than two billion people, with the youngest population on the planet. It is the last continent with significant demographic expansion. Where China is aging and Europe is shrinking, Africa is growing. From Beijing's perspective, this is not a statistical curiosity: it is a strategic lever. Whoever builds the Africa of the future — its energy grids, its infrastructure, its cities, its digital platforms — will hold an unprecedented position of influence over coming generations.

China is the only major power that has understood this clearly. It does not merely invest in roads, ports, and railways; it invests in leadership classes, school curricula, universities, digital media. It offers scholarships, builds military academies, trains civil servants. It has developed a diplomatic model that treats African nations not as marginal entities, but as political partners. There is no European paternalism, no Western conditionality: there is recognition. And it is here that part of Africa's fascination with China is born: China does not evangelize; it presents itself.

The second element is the material dimension. China already controls a vast share of Africa's infrastructure: power plants, ports, highways, rail systems. But this does not mean Africa is "captured" in a colonial sense: it means China has understood the most obvious thing the West has forgotten — that without infrastructure there is no development. The West stopped building long ago; China has begun building everywhere. And this asymmetry is not technical: it is geopolitical.

The third element is debt diplomacy. As with the BRI, Chinese loans in Africa are neither acts of charity nor explicit tools of coercion: they are contracts of influence. Indebted countries know that China will not impose democratic conditionality or unpopular reforms; they also know that renegotiation is possible if needed. But the exchange is clear: diplomatic support. This is why, in international institutions, China can count on broad African backing. It is the result of a strategy built over twenty years of dense presence, not of threats.

The fourth element is the most unsettling, because it is the one Jin does not see or does not want to see: Africa is the perfect laboratory for Chinese political technologies. Surveillance systems, digital platforms, 5G networks, smart cities, biometric identification — China exports technology and, with it, a model of governance. It does not sell just cameras: it sells integrated control systems. It does not sell just software: it sells security infrastructures. And this creates a deep dependency: technical, political, institutional. A dependency that, over time, orients domestic politics in adopting countries toward models more compatible with China's digital authoritarianism.

The fifth element concerns the West. Europe and the United States continue to speak of Africa as if it were a continent seeking help. China, instead, speaks to Africa as a continent seeking a role. It is an enormous difference. Europe offers conditions; China offers opportunities. Europe asks for guarantees; China asks for collaboration. Europe sees risk; China sees potential. And while Europeans debate, China builds. And while the United States oscillates between attention and disinterest, China deepens its relationships.

This dynamic has a name: historical anticipation. Jin depicts China as a country that reacts; in Africa, China does not react at all: it anticipates. It sees what the West no longer sees. It speaks to a rising continent while the West speaks to declining ones. This is not simply an economic issue: it is a matter of geopolitical imagination.

Africa is the game of the century because it is where three decisive dynamics converge: demographic growth, infrastructural void, and technological competition. Whoever becomes Africa's dominant partner will hold a strategic advantage for the entire twenty-first century. China is already on the field. The West is not.

And Jin, in her "economic" analysis, fails to see the elephant in the room: China is not building bridges; it is building historical alliances. It is not importing raw materials; it is importing international legitimacy. It is not exporting engineering; it is exporting power.

To understand Africa is to understand China's project. And that is why Africa is the missing chapter in Jin's book: too strategic to be read with technical tools, too decisive to be left to the metaphors of development. Africa is the future, and China knows it.

PART IV

AGAINST JIN, WITH JIN: A CRITICAL PATH

The Merits of China That the West Does Not Want to See

DISENCHANTMENT WITH THE WESTERN IDEA OF THE MARKET

One of the most intelligent — and most uncomfortable — points in Jin's book is her invitation to reconsider our almost metaphysical faith in the market as a universal coordination mechanism. It is neither an ideological attack nor a praise of dirigisme; rather, it is an invitation to disenchantment. Jin argues that many Western criticisms of the "Chinese model" arise from an implicit assumption: that there is only one correct way to organize an economy, and that this way coincides with free competition, regulatory transparency, and state neutrality. China, in Jin's view, does not violate a principle: it simply applies another paradigm. And sometimes — this is the part the West struggles to accept — it works better.

This observation deserves to be taken seriously. The West has built a cult around the market, turning it into a place of truth: what succeeds is true, what fails is false. But the Western market has never been neutral: it has always been guided by political choices, regulatory interventions, sectoral protections, and state decisions disguised as competitive dynamics. The idea of "pure" capitalism is an ideological construction, not a fact. Jin forces us to acknowledge this, and she does so with an honesty the West rarely applies to itself.

For years, China produced extraordinary growth rates not because it imitated the West, but because it built an imperfect, directed, manipulated — and yet highly effective — market. It used the state as an accelerator, as a corrector, as an industrial promoter. It controlled credit prices, steered investment flows, and created entire industrial sectors from scratch. And it had the courage — which the West has lost — to intervene where markets failed: to build infrastructure, orient technological development, and bridge regional divides.

This does not mean that the Chinese model is superior or desirable; it means that the West has been telling itself a fairy tale for decades: that the market, if left alone, always produces order, innovation, and prosperity. 2008 disproved this. The stagnation of the middle class disproved it. The climate crisis disproved it. And Jin has the merit of reminding us: the market is not a moral guarantee; it is a tool. And the state is not an intruder: it is an integral part of the game.

Jin strikes a nerve when she describes the Western obsession with the neutrality of the state. In the Western narrative, the state must be an umpire, not a player; a regulator, not a strategist. But over the past twenty years, the opposite of this narrative has happened: China has become both player and referee, while the West convinced itself it could remain a spectator. The result is that China built enormous industrial capacities — from batteries to solar panels, from high-speed rail to telecommunications — while Europe and the United States allowed entire sectors to collapse for "lack of competitiveness."

The question Jin implicitly poses to the West is simple: what stops you from using the state as a strategic lever? It is not an invitation to authoritarianism; it is an invitation to reclaim the economic sovereignty the West abandoned out of ideological loyalty to laissez-faire. Jin shows that, in the face of global crises, the market without political intervention is too slow, too short-sighted, too fragile.

Another merit of her analysis is that she recognizes something many Western economists overlook: the Chinese population never believed in the liberal promise. For the Chinese middle class, the state is not the enemy of the market: it is the guarantor of the market. It is the perimeter within which economic life can unfold without sliding into chaos. For decades, the Party's stability was perceived as the enabling condition for individual enrichment. And this is something the West struggles to grasp: in China, economic freedom is not conceived as emancipation *from* the state, but *with* the state.

In this sense Jin makes an important contribution: she dismantles the idea that China is a pathological exception. If anything, it is the West that convinced itself that one universal model exists. Jin forces us to see China as another possible way of organizing modernity — not necessarily better, but real, functional, capable of results the West is no longer able to achieve.

This does not mean embracing the Party's political narrative or ignoring the risks and costs of the model: authoritarianism, opacity, structural inefficiencies, financial fragilities, social control. But it does mean acknowledging that, in criticizing those risks, the West cannot hide behind the ideological arrogance of believing its own system is naturally superior.

One of Jin's most solid merits is precisely this: reminding the West that it does not hold a monopoly on economic rationality or historical efficiency. It is an uncomfortable lesson, but a necessary one. And to face China lucidly — criticizing when needed, cooperating when possible, competing when inevitable — the West must first free itself from its own illusions about the market. Jin helps us do that.

FORMS OF STABILITY THAT ARE NOT REPRESSION

One of the subtlest and most compelling passages in Jin's book concerns the distinction between political stability and repression. The West, observing China from the outside, tends to conflate the two immediately: if a regime is not democratic, then every form of stability must by definition be the result of coercion. Jin instead urges us to distinguish. Not because repression does not exist — it certainly does, and on a vast scale — but because it is not sufficient to explain the depth and endurance of China's social cohesion. To understand the real China, one must acknowledge that there are forms of stability that do not stem from fear but from cultural, social, psychological, and even economic factors that the West struggles to perceive.

The first element is cultural continuity. In China, social cohesion is not constructed solely from above: it is rooted in long history. The idea of harmony, the preference for order, the distrust of chaos, the centrality of the family as the primary safety net, the valuing of education as a path to mobility — all of these predate the current regime by centuries. The Party exploits them, certainly, but it does not create them. There is a collective predisposition to view stability as a positive value, not a forced imposition. The West tends to interpret this predisposition as resignation; Jin interprets it as a genuine collective preference — and she is, at least in part, correct.

The second element is the legitimacy of growth. For thirty years, China delivered a material improvement unprecedented in human history. Hundreds of millions of people rose out of poverty, cities expanded explosively, opportunities multiplied, and social mobility was real. Stability did not stem from fear of protesting, but from the conviction that the system worked. A society experiencing rapid, tangible improvement tends naturally to support the order that enables it. This is not repression; it is practical rationality. It is the "implicit social contract" that Jin describes better than any Western observer.

The third element is administrative efficiency. Despite its limits and opacity, Chinese governance has achieved administrative results that many Western democracies can no longer manage: building infrastructure quickly, managing urban density, reducing certain forms of crime, maintaining a relatively competent bureaucracy. In many parts of China, the perception of a capable state generates stability not out of fear, but out of pragmatic trust: if the system works, you don't change the system.

The fourth element — perhaps the most underestimated — is family cohesion as a social buffer. In China, the extended family largely replaces the welfare state: it supports young people, absorbs unemployment, and takes care of the elderly. This creates an informal safety net that softens social conflict. It is a form of stability that has nothing to do with repression and everything to do with the anthropological structure of society. In the West, weaker family networks make protest more likely because vulnerability is more individual; in China, vulnerability is more collective, distributed within the family, and thus less inclined to erupt politically.

The fifth element is symbolic mobility. Even when real mobility slows — as is happening today — Chinese society continues to be sustained by a cultural expectation of progress: education, sacrifice, self-improvement. This belief in the possibility of advancement generates patience and discipline. The West interprets this patience as passivity. Jin suggests instead that it is a form of deferred intentionality: the sense that life can improve not here and now, but across the generational cycle.

None of this, of course, erases the reality of repression: it exists, it weighs heavily, it constrains, and it defines the boundaries of the possible. But Jin is right to argue that Chinese stability cannot be explained solely by repression. Reducing a country of 1.4 billion people to a mere product of coercion is an intellectual shortcut that prevents us from seeing what truly sustains the system. China is not stable only because dissent is punished; it is stable because millions of people, for a long time, perceived that system as functional, effective, and capable of improving their lives.

And yet — and here my analysis diverges from Jin's — these very forms of "non-repressive" stability are now more fragile than they once were. Growth is slowing, social mobility is stalling, the family is under demographic strain, the state is becoming more intrusive, administrative trust is fraying. The risk is not that repression will increase — that has already happened — but that the positive foundations of stability will erode, leaving as the sole remaining adhesive precisely what Jin seeks to downplay: fear.

Jin's merit is showing that Chinese stability is not an illusion; Jin's limit is failing to see how that same stability has entered a delicate phase. Understanding this tension — between what the system has built and what it now risks losing — is one of the keys to interpreting the China to come.

CHINA AS A LIVING CRITIQUE OF NEOLIBERALISM

Among the most fertile — and most provocative — insights in Jin's book is the idea that China represents, willingly or not, a living critique of Western neoliberalism. Not a theoretical critique, like that offered by heterodox economists, social movements, or philosophers; not a moral critique, like those denouncing inequality; but a historical critique embodied in a functioning alternative model. China has not disproved neoliberalism with a manifesto: it has disproved it by building an economy that, while violating almost all its dogmas, has achieved results no contemporary liberal economy has come close to matching.

It is a point the West tends to suppress because it is uncomfortable. And it is a point Jin identifies with clarity, even if she does not fully draw out its political implications.

The first critique China directs at neoliberalism is pragmatic: it shows that markets do not self-regulate, do not spontaneously distribute prosperity, do not build infrastructure on their own, do not correct territorial imbalances. For twenty years the West believed that the retreat of the state would unleash productive energies. China did the exact opposite: an omnipresent, dirigiste, interventionist, sometimes heavy-handed state, yet one capable of steering the economy toward long-term goals. Neoliberalism privatized; China planned. And the historical outcome — however accompanied by enormous costs — was the greatest economic development ever recorded.

The second critique concerns time. Neoliberalism reasons in the short term: quarters, financial flows, market reactions. China reasons in the long term: historical cycles, generations, infrastructure designed for 2070, not for this year's budget. Its investment logic — often inefficient in the short run — is extremely powerful over time. Neoliberalism, in its cult of liquidity, disinvested from the future; China, in its cult of continuity, built a material future. Western development became increasingly immaterial, financial, volatile; Chinese development was physical, concrete, accumulative. And in the real world, made of land, networks, ports, mines, electricity, factories, the winner is the one who accumulates infrastructure, not the one who optimizes portfolios.

The third critique is social. Neoliberalism has accepted — at times even embraced — rising inequality as an inevitable by-product of efficiency. China, though a very unequal society, made upward mobility an ideological pillar: no one was meant to remain behind forever. The Chinese promise was brutally simple: *work, study, save, and you will live better than your parents.* For decades it proved true. The West, by contrast, produced widespread middle-class stagnation. It is no accident that many European and American societies now look at China with a mix of fascination and fear: China shows what they can no longer achieve.

The fourth critique is institutional. Neoliberalism built a minimal state that hesitates to intervene in the economy; China built a maximal state that does not fear shaping entire sectors. The West interprets this as "interference in the market"; China interprets it as "market creation." It is a radical difference. Many of the strategic industries of the twenty-first century — batteries, solar power, telecommunications, artificial intelligence — emerged in China not *despite* the state, but *because of* the state. The West continues to believe that innovation is the child of individual freedom; China shows it can also be the child of collective direction.

The fifth — and deepest — critique is philosophical. Neoliberalism is an ideology of the individual: each person maximizes their own interest, and from this aggregation emerges order. China is an ideology of the collective: order is produced by central direction, and the individual finds freedom within that framework. The West built modernity on the idea that the market replaces political will; China built its modernity on the idea that political will replaces the market. This is not only economics: it is an opposing metaphysics.

And it is precisely here that my reading diverges from Jin's. Jin describes China as an economic alternative; but in reality China is an anthropological alternative. It does not simply propose a model of development, but a model of the relationship between individual, society, and state. Neoliberalism sees the individual as the starting point; China sees the individual as the end point. In this sense China is not the critique of neoliberalism: it is its antithesis.

But this does not mean China is right. It means neoliberalism has lost its power to convince — not because it was contested ideologically, but because it was disproved materially. China shows that alternative ways of building prosperity exist; that the market is not infallible; that the state, if competent, can be a driver of development; that globalization does not necessarily produce democracy; that modernity does not come in a single form.

This is the part of Jin's argument the West should hear without arrogance: China is not an accident; it is a refutation. Not of political liberalism — which does not exist in China — but of economic liberalism. Not a theoretical refutation, but a historical one.

The point, however, is that Jin sees only the bright side of this critique. I also see the dark side: the concentration of power, the ossification of creativity, the aging of society, the slowing of growth, the rising of fear. Neoliberalism has been disproved; the Chinese model has not yet been confirmed.

China is a living critique of neoliberalism, but not yet an answer. And this is why it deserves to be studied without submission and without hubris. Identifying what China reveals — and what China ignores — is one of the most urgent intellectual tasks of our time.

The Illusions About China That Jin Cannot Admit

THE FRAGILITY OF THE SOCIAL CONTRACT

Jin describes China's social contract as one of the country's great strengths: an implicit agreement between state and citizens based on growth, stability, and material improvement. For thirty years, this contract worked with astonishing efficiency. But what Jin cannot say openly — and what many Chinese analysts understand perfectly well — is that this contract now creaks. Not because it has been broken, but because the historical conditions that made it possible have faded.

To understand this fragility, one must start from the nature of the contract itself. In its official version, the Party promises three things: continuous development, social order, and collective protection from global uncertainty. In exchange, it asks for two things: avoidance of political chaos and support for national direction. It is a functional contract, not an ideological one; material rather than symbolic. But precisely for this reason it is vulnerable: it rests on verifiable promises. As long as life improves, the promise is credible. When life stops improving, the contract becomes a question mark.

The first point of fragility is the end of automatic growth. After decades of double-digit development, China is entering a period of structural slowdown. Not a temporary negative cycle, but a permanent shift in the country's trajectory: declining population, stagnant productivity, a real-estate crisis, accumulated inefficiencies, public investments with diminishing returns. The implicit message is devastating: growth can no longer be taken for granted. And if growth is the foundation of the social contract, its erosion undermines the entire architecture of consent.

The second point of fragility is blocked social mobility. For two generations, young Chinese believed in a better future. Education was the springboard, the city the space of opportunity, effort a sensible investment. Today that narrative no longer works. Urbanisation is nearly complete, the labour market is saturated, competition is fierce, demographic decline narrows career horizons, and property is no longer a reliable path to wealth. While Jin celebrates "resilience," a new and troubling sentiment spreads instead: the sense that the social climb leads nowhere. The *tang ping* generation — "lying flat" — is not apathetic; it is disillusioned.

The third point of fragility is the economic insecurity of households. The Chinese miracle was financed by private savings: families who put aside everything for housing, education, and elder care. But today financial pressure is explosive: the cost of schooling, the cost of care, the cost of urban life, the cost of housing. The promise of a prosperous future confronts a reality made of psychological and material precarity. Families — once a driver of stability — become potential vectors of social anxiety.

The fourth point is the crisis of trust. Not in the Party — which remains strong and omnipresent — but in expectations. The Shanghai lockdown, the rigid Covid-era restrictions, the opaque handling of local economic crises, the repression of spontaneous cultural phenomena: all these have undermined the perception that the state is always competent, always benevolent, always able to correct its own mistakes. Jin describes an "adaptive," reactive, dynamic state. Today that image is no longer obvious. Cracks in public management turn into cracks in legitimacy.

The fifth point of fragility is the question Jin does not want to confront: what holds a country together when material promises are no longer credible? For China does not have an ideological contract — not anymore — nor a coherent civil religion. The People's Republic lives on pragmatism, not transcendence. When pragmatism falters, what replaces it? Jin cannot ask this question openly, because it implies the possibility of political tension — a possibility the official narrative does not allow.

China's social contract was the most effective in the contemporary world, but also the most conditional: it depended on infinite growth in a finite world, on permanent upward mobility in an increasingly rigid society, on constant administrative competence in a system that is becoming more rigid and less meritocratic. Its fragilities are not accidents: they are structural.

And this brings us to the central point that Jin cannot admit. Chinese stability is not in imminent danger — the Party still possesses enormous tools of control, consent, and legitimacy — but its nature is changing. Less and less stability *because* the system works; more and more stability *because* the system cannot be questioned. And this is a silent but fundamental transition: stability based on expectation turns into stability based on constraint.

Jin cannot say it; I can. The fragility of the social contract is not the prelude to collapse — China is not on the verge of exploding — but the prelude to a transformation in the form of its stability. A stability that is less economic and more political.

Only by recognising this fragility — without exaggerating it, without denying it — can we understand the China that is emerging: less optimistic, more rigid; less confident, more anxious. A China that Jin cannot afford to describe in full — but one that stands in the background of every page of her book.

THE STAGNATION OF PRODUCTIVITY

Among all the fragilities of the Chinese model, the one Jin touches upon but does not address with the necessary depth is perhaps the most structural: the stagnation of productivity. It is an extremely delicate topic, because it calls into question the very core of the Chinese miracle — not its speed, but its sustainability. As long as productivity rises, China can continue to compensate for its imbalances; once productivity stalls, everything else begins to creak: debt, demography, public investment, innovation. And that is precisely what is happening.

Jin describes this phenomenon as a physiological slowdown, predictable in an economy that has already caught up technologically in the easier sectors. But the issue runs deeper. China is not experiencing a natural evolution; it is experiencing a structural blockage. The model that generated forty years of growth is running out because it was built on elements that no longer exist: a young and expanding labour force, a state capable of channeling physical investment that truly increased output, a dynamic private sector able to innovate without being constrained by political considerations. Every single element of that system is now under pressure.

The first obstacle is demographic. A rapidly aging population produces less, saves less, innovates less, and consumes less dynamically. Productivity is not merely a technical metric: it is the product of social energy. China once had a vast young and disciplined workforce; today it has a shrinking labour force and a younger generation that is more educated but smaller, more ambitious but less incentivized. Innovation becomes harder when demographic structure pulls you downward.

The second obstacle is urban. Urbanisation — both a blessing and a curse of the Chinese miracle — is now approaching its limit. For decades, moving millions from countryside to city automatically increased productivity: every transfer was a leap toward more complex, better-paid, more efficient work. But now that resource is exhausted. There will never again be tens of millions of rural migrants ready to fuel urban growth. Moreover, Chinese cities have reached levels of logistical and environmental saturation that make marginal improvements increasingly costly.

The third obstacle — the one Jin almost entirely avoids — is political. Chinese productivity is not slowing only for economic reasons; it is slowing because the Party-state has compromised some of the mechanisms that made it possible. The private tech sector, the beating heart of China's innovation for years, has been hit by sudden and punitive regulatory campaigns: antitrust crackdowns on digital giants, restrictions on private tutoring, fintech containment, zero-Covid policies that paralysed businesses and consumers. The message to companies has been clear: growth is conditional on political conformity. This strengthens control but weakens productivity. Innovation requires risk, experimentation, eccentricity — and these do not survive well in an environment where mistakes can be interpreted as disloyalty.

The fourth obstacle is the quality of investment. For twenty years, China built infrastructure that truly increased productivity: roads, ports, railways, energy plants, factories, industrial zones. Today, however, a significant share of public investment flows into projects that do not generate proportional added value: empty stadiums, underused airports, uninhabited residential complexes, railway lines that are economically unsustainable. The investment multiplier has collapsed. The result is a paradox: China invests more than any country in the world, but gets less and less out of each yuan invested.

The fifth obstacle is the incentive system. For years, local officials were motivated by a simple rule: economic growth = promotion. This generated excesses, distortions, even corruption, but also created an extraordinary administrative dynamism. Today this mechanism has been replaced by another: political stability = promotion. Growth matters, but obedience matters more. Political priority has replaced economic ambition. The result is a more cautious bureaucracy, less innovative, less willing to take risks. This, too, directly depresses productivity.

Jin treats productivity as if it were a technical issue, solvable through better industrial policy, more education, more R&D. But the root of the problem is not technical: it is systemic. Productivity stagnates because the Chinese political-economic model is shifting direction: increasingly oriented toward control and decreasingly toward dynamism. When China was running fast, it could afford a certain degree of economic freedom. But when growth slows, the Party naturally moves to tighten control.

It is a mechanism of self-preservation. And as always happens in non-democratic systems, political security takes precedence over economic efficiency.

This is what Jin cannot say: the stagnation of productivity is not an accident, but a symptom. A symptom of the transition from a China opening to the world to a China closing in on itself; from a China that experimented to a China that fears risk; from a China that grew because it could, to a China that slows because it must preserve stability.

The real question, then, is not how to increase productivity, but whether China can do so without giving up its current degree of political control. And that is a question Jin does not answer — because to answer it, she would have to interrogate the core of the system.

I, instead, can say it plainly: China will be able to increase its productivity only if it finds a way to release energies that are now being held down. And in a system that prioritizes obedience, the energy of innovation is always the first to dim.

THE TOTAL SECURITY TRAP

Among the truths Jin does not address — and that no economist can truly integrate without turning her analysis into a political treatise — is the one that defines the deepest and most dangerous condition in which China finds itself today: the trap of total security. It is the classic paradox of modern authoritarian systems: the more they strengthen themselves to guarantee stability, the more they generate the conditions of their own fragility.

Contemporary China does not simply have a generic "security problem"; it has a problem of hyper-security: a growing, almost totalizing obsession with political, social, informational, technological, and even psychological control. This obsession arises from a real fear — that economic slowdown, geopolitical tensions, technological competition, and international pressure may undermine the Party's power. But in confronting these challenges, the system evolves in a way that makes it more compact, more rigid, more nervous. A power that fears risk too much eventually suffocates the very sources of its vitality.

The first layer of the trap concerns the economic sphere. In a climate of total security, every company — from the major tech platforms to the smallest entrepreneurs — must continually demonstrate political loyalty. Strategic decisions are no longer taken to maximize productivity but to minimize exposure to suspicion. Innovation, by definition risky, deviant, unpredictable, becomes a potentially ambiguous act. The result is a system that is less creative, more cautious, more conformist. What Jin celebrates as "adaptive governance" becomes, in reality, defensive governance. And it is precisely when the economy slows that control tends to expand, creating a feedback loop: less growth → more fear → more control → less innovation → even less growth.

The second layer is informational. Total security requires an environment in which surprises are minimized. Yet surprises are often what allow a system to adapt: criticism, exposed errors, bottom-up feedback, open discussion, conflict of ideas. In today's hyper-monitored China, the circulation of information is tightly filtered. This creates apparent stability and real instability: the leadership has access only to pre-processed information, often sugar-coated, always politically decoded. A system that can no longer hear its own body becomes deaf to its warning signals. Total security produces selective blindness.

The third layer is social. After 2020, China vastly expanded its capacity for control: health codes, tracking systems, facial recognition, movement restrictions, digital platforms integrated with the political system. Even when many measures were lifted, the infrastructure of control remained. This changes collective psychology. A society that perceives every space as monitored does not develop horizontal trust, community spirit, or social initiative. Total security does not produce community; it produces generalized caution. A cautious population is stable — as long as nothing aggravates it. But when trust in the system begins to crack, caution turns into silent frustration, and silent frustration is a deeper form of instability than visible protest.

The fourth layer is institutional. In a system obsessed with security, local officials have an overwhelming incentive to avoid any political risk. Suddenly, what was once rewarded — experimentation, pragmatism, initiative — becomes potentially dangerous. The career dynamic changes: boldness becomes recklessness, caution becomes virtue. The result is a bureaucracy that does not make mistakes because it does not act. A China that does not make mistakes may appear efficient; in reality, it is a China that does not learn.

The fifth layer is international. China sees threats everywhere: in American technology, in global supply chains, in Asian alliances, in multilateral institutions. Some threats are real; others are projections of domestic vulnerability. But total security on the external front produces an obvious effect: closure. And closure, for a country whose miracle was built on openness, is a slow form of self-weakening. An isolated China is less innovative, less attractive, less informed, less influential. Total security abroad reduces real power at home.

The trap lies in this vicious cycle: the more China seeks stability through control, the more it weakens the sources of stability; the more it weakens the sources of stability, the more it feels compelled to increase control. It is a psychological mechanism before it is a political one.

Jin, as an economist and a figure recognized both inside and outside China, cannot address this knot. Her analysis must necessarily stop a millimetre before acknowledging the link between economic slowdown and increased political control. But this omission does not make the problem less real — it makes it more acute.

Total security is a rational response to a world perceived as hostile. But it is also, paradoxically, an unproductive strategy for a country that needs flexibility, creativity, and trust to navigate the most difficult transition of the last forty years.

China is not at risk of collapse; it is at risk of something subtler and more enduring: the slow erosion of its historical energy. And this erosion does not come from protests or dissidents, but from what power fears most of all: the stagnation of innovation, the loss of initiative, the transformation of social vitality into conformism. This is the total security trap.

It is what Jin cannot say — but what is essential to understanding the China that is coming.

A General Theory of State Capitalism

COMPARISON WITH SOUTH KOREA, JAPAN, AND SINGAPORE

To truly understand the nature of China's state capitalism — and to avoid confusing it either with socialist planning or with an authoritarian variant of Western capitalism — it is essential to place it within a broader genealogy: the tradition of state-led industrialization in East Asia. South Korea, Japan, and Singapore represent three archetypes of successful state capitalism. Each of these models produced extraordinary results in terms of growth, innovation, and human development. And yet, none of them truly resembles China. The comparison highlights what China shares with these precedents and, above all, what makes it irreducible to any of them.

The first point of comparison is postwar Japan. Its Ministry of International Trade and Industry (MITI) was for decades the most sophisticated industrial-policy laboratory in the world. It coordinated credit, technology, competition, and export markets; identified strategic sectors; and protected national champions until they reached maturity. China uses similar tools: preferential credit, state-owned enterprises as pillars, sectoral planning, state–business collaboration. But the resemblance ends there. Japan operated in a democratic context, albeit with a dominant LDP; more importantly, it operated within an international order guaranteed by the United States, which ensured external security and open markets. Japan did not need to compete for global leadership: it needed to prosper within a system that posed no existential threat. China, by contrast, is not merely developing within the existing order: it seeks to reshape it. Its industrial policy is not simply optimization; it is a quest for strategic emancipation. This is the gap Jin underestimates.

The second model is South Korea. As in China, the state guided growth through conglomerates (the chaebol), targeted protection, early repression of organized labor, and disciplined credit allocation. But Korea made a transition that China has not yet faced: democratization. Beginning in the 1980s, South Korea discovered something many economists are reluctant to acknowledge: advanced capitalism needs political freedoms, transparency, regulated conflict, and pluralism in economic decision-making. That transition profoundly altered the behavior of the chaebol, improved governance, and reduced corruption. China, instead, is moving in the opposite direction: not toward political opening, but toward its contraction. And this is no detail: state capitalism can produce miracles in the accumulation phase, but without institutional pluralism it tends to suffocate in the innovation phase. Here the comparison is not favorable to China.

The third model is Singapore: a small, hyper-technocratic country built on an extraordinary fusion of social discipline, a state-as-entrepreneur, and international openness. It is the favorite model of China's admirers, as it shows that a not-fully-democratic regime can be efficient, innovative, wealthy, and stable. But Singapore is irreproducible: a city-state, ethnically diverse yet geographically tiny, deeply integrated into global circuits, governed by an authority that — though authoritarian — has never been totalizing. The People's Action Party has never sought — nor could it have sought — to control every sector of social life as the Chinese Communist Party does. Singapore is paternalistic and meritocratic state capitalism; China is centralized state capitalism subordinated to a single party that accepts no external limits. The comparison serves mainly to show what China is not: a neutral technocratic system. Its state capitalism has always been, from the beginning, a specific form of political power.

Now, the similarities. All three of these countries used the state to:

- protect infant industries;
- coordinate private and public investment;

- plan firmly yet pragmatically;
- negotiate with foreign capital from a position of strength;
- create large conglomerates able to compete globally.

These elements are present in China as well, and Jin describes them accurately. But what Jin does not say is that China has introduced two features never seen in any of these models.

The first is scale. China is not a country; it is a continent. Its state capitalism operates over a population of 1.4 billion people, with regions larger than entire European states. No previous model can be transposed onto this scale without being radically transformed.

The second is political depth. In Chinese state capitalism it is not the state that guides the economy: it is the Party–state. This changes everything. The Japanese, Korean, and Singaporean models are technocratic; the Chinese model is partitocratic. The logic guiding decisions is not merely economic, nor simply national: it is political in the strongest sense, because it is tied to the survival and primacy of the Chinese Communist Party.

In other words: Chinese state capitalism is not an Asian variant of the Japanese model; it is not a giant version of the Korean model; it is not a continental Singapore. It is an entirely new experiment, combining for the first time in human history:

- sectoral planning on an imperial scale;
- state-owned enterprises as political instruments;
- private companies as conditioned extensions of the Party;
- ideological centralization;
- global geopolitical ambitions.

This combination yields extraordinary results, but also risks that Jin does not address: accumulated financial fragilities, increasing rigidity, constrained innovation, dependence on central political decisions, and difficulty correcting systemic errors.

The point is not that Chinese state capitalism will fail. The point is that it cannot be evaluated using the same analytical framework as previous models. It is something new, and therefore unstable: powerful yet exposed; efficient yet fragile; modern yet anchored to a political logic that limits its evolution.

The comparison with Japan, Korea, and Singapore leads to a single conclusion: China is the only country to have attempted to transform state capitalism into a global project of power. And as long as Jin describes it only in its economic dimension, she will inevitably miss the most important part of the story.

THE LOGIC OF SCALE: WHEN THE MODEL WORKS AND WHEN IT IMPLODES

Scale is the hidden key behind everything China has accomplished over the past forty years. It is not simply a dimension but a logic: a way of conceiving development, political action, modernization, and even the imagination of the future. China did not become powerful because it is large; it became large because it learned how to transform its immensity into an engine of growth. For decades, this logic worked almost flawlessly: a vast country with a growing mass of workers, savings, administrative capacity, and a Party able to mobilize all of this in a single direction. Scale was a flywheel: the more you invested, the more you produced; the more people moved to the cities, the higher productivity rose; the more you built, the faster you grew. The Chinese model was simple and immensely powerful: do a great deal, on a massive scale, very quickly.

China was inimitable for precisely this reason. Every lever was amplified: the availability of labor, the concentration of political power, the accumulation of capital, urbanization, infrastructure construction. The West looked at this gigantism with suspicion, but underestimated its efficiency. Move fifteen million people a year from the countryside to the cities and productivity rises automatically. Build thousands of kilometers of railways, ports, power plants, and logistics transforms—bringing entire sectors along with it. China did not do complex things; it did simple things in such quantities that they generated systemic effects. It was an economy of mass in the most literal sense.

But scale is not a neutral virtue: it is a substance that reacts differently depending on the context. The same force that allows a system to accelerate can, over time, become the force that pulls it downward. This is precisely what is happening to China — and what Jin cannot say explicitly. The scale model only works when there are still masses to mobilize, territories to urbanize, infrastructure to build, incomes to double, flows of people and capital to direct. When this phase ends, scale stops being an advantage and begins to turn into a constraint.

Demography is the clearest example: a huge population can be an extraordinary engine when it is growing, but a powerful brake when it is aging. China has now entered the second phase: the same number of people who once represented a competitive advantage has become a social, healthcare, and economic burden. Urbanization, which was the greatest productivity accelerator in modern history, has also turned into a problem of overcapacity: cities that are too large, empty housing, public investment that no longer generates growth but costs. The scale of debt — both local and national — is now too large to be absorbed by rising productivity: it requires a kind of qualitative growth the current system struggles to produce.

Politics amplifies this mechanism. When scale was a strength, centralization was an advantage: one command, one direction, one objective. But now that the country needs innovation, experimentation, flexibility, centralization becomes a constraint. The scale of decision-making is too large for the system to correct itself quickly; too controlled for dissent to reveal errors;

too rigid for creativity to emerge without suspicion. A massive country that grows rigid resembles a gigantic body losing flexibility: every movement becomes slower, every deviation more dangerous, every mistake more costly.

Scale, in short, works when growth is extensive: when simply adding more inputs — more workers, more capital, more land, more urbanization — produces more output. It implodes when growth must become intensive: when you must extract more from what you already have, innovate instead of replicate, improve instead of accumulate. This is the hardest transition for any economy, but for a continental-scale economy like China it is almost an anthropological leap.

And here emerges what Jin does not state openly. China does not risk an explosive crisis; it risks something slower and deeper: the inability to transform its scale into quality. The country learned how to grow by replicating; it must now learn how to grow by transforming. This requires economic freedom, administrative pluralism, unauthorized creativity, real competition — all elements that the political logic of total security tends to compress.

The problem is not that scale has become useless; the problem is that China can no longer use it in the old way. For the first time in forty years, quantity is no longer enough. And until China shifts from a logic of accumulation to a logic of transformation, its very vastness risks becoming a burden. This is the contradiction Jin avoids and that, in fact, defines China's new era: the scale that once propelled China forward now anchors it to a model that can no longer function as before. Here is where the miracle meets its limit. And from here it will have to begin again.

THE THEORETICAL CONTRIBUTION THIS BOOK CAN MAKE

At this point, it is necessary to clarify the deeper meaning of a work like this. It is not simply a matter of responding to Jin, nor of refuting her optimism, nor of expanding her analysis with political, historical, or geopolitical elements that—out of necessity or prudence—remain implicit in her book. The point is something else: to propose a general theory capable of reading China not as an exception, nor as a threat, nor as a model, but as a historical crossroads where the crises and possibilities of the twenty-first century converge.

The potential contribution of this book, if it exists, lies in its ability to do what neither the West nor China itself fully manages to do: to recognize simultaneously the power and the limits of the Chinese model; to see in the same object both its transformative energy and its structural fragility. The West tends to oscillate between fascination and fear: either it celebrates China as a new paradigm, or it demonizes it as an existential threat. China, for its part, tends to present itself as an unstoppable force. In both cases, the essential theoretical dimension is lost: China is not a destiny, but a particular form that global capitalism takes when it passes through a centralized political system, a millennial history, and an unprecedented scale.

This book can therefore make a contribution on three levels.

The first is conceptual. China is not simply state capitalism, nor authoritarian capitalism, nor post-socialism. It is a new combination: a form of political capitalism driven by a ruling party, capable of generating extraordinary development as long as it operates within an extensive-growth framework, but destined to encounter profound challenges the moment growth must become qualitative. No Western category is sufficient to describe it, just as no Chinese category can fully justify it. The theoretical task, therefore, is to elaborate a new interpretative grid: to understand China not as a deviation, but as a possibility internal to capitalism itself.

The second level is historical-structural. China reveals something the West has forgotten: that economic development is not a natural process but a political construction; that the state is not only a regulator but also a creator of markets; that growth does not arise from spontaneity but from intentionality. This does not mean that the Chinese model is desirable or superior, but it does mean that the liberal dichotomy between state and market is theoretically insufficient. China shows, with the concreteness of facts, that capitalism is always hybrid, always political, always institutionally situated. And this revelation belongs not only to China: it belongs to the world emerging after globalization.

The third level is critical. China is a living critique of neoliberalism, but also a living critique of the limits of technological authoritarianism. It is a system that has shown that growth can be politically directed, but has also shown that innovation suffers wherever society fears making mistakes. It is a system that has reduced poverty and illiteracy at record speed, yet has created new forms of social anxiety, psychological fragility, and existential constraint. It is a system that lifted hundreds of millions out of poverty, but must now manage a population that no longer accepts material well-being as sufficient. The theoretical contribution of this book lies in holding these two sides together: China as possibility and China as warning.

Finally, there is a less theoretical but perhaps more urgent contribution: language. Speaking about China often means slipping into the register of propaganda, polemic, or admiration. Here the task is instead to restore complexity: to recognize what works without censoring what worries us; to acknowledge what China can teach without falling into superficial imitation; to understand what China reveals about the world without assigning it a messianic or destabilizing role.

In this sense, this book can offer something rarely found in public debate: a place where China is treated neither as threat nor as salvation, but as an intellectual challenge that forces us to rethink our idea of development, power, security, and freedom. A challenge that concerns not only China, but also—and perhaps above all—the West observing it.

The theoretical contribution, then, does not consist in proposing an alternative model, but in clarifying what the Chinese model reveals: that the future of capitalism will depend on three unresolved tensions — between scale and quality, between control and creativity, between stability and legitimacy. It is within these tensions that the fate of China — and with it, much of the world — will be decided.

Conclusion

Reaching the end of this journey, it becomes clear that the central question is no longer: *Will China win or lose?* That is a superficial, almost childish question. China is not a competitor in a race; it is a historical laboratory, and what happens within it anticipates many of the tensions that will soon concern the world at large.

Those who observe China only to predict triumph or collapse doom themselves to misunderstanding it. The point is not whether China will continue to grow, but *how* it will grow and at what cost; not whether its model will survive, but whether it will manage to transform itself; not whether its state capitalism is better or worse than its Western counterpart, but what both models reveal about the possibilities and limits of capitalism itself.

If this book has a purpose, it is precisely to show that China cannot be reduced to either threat or promise. It is a system that has demonstrated extraordinary coordinating capacity, yet risks suffocating under the weight of its own control; a system that has generated growth like no other, yet now sees that growth slowing; a system that built stability not only through repression but through real improvements in people's lives, and that now must reckon with a social contract more fragile than it appears. It is a system that made scale its strength, and now faces the risk of being crushed by it.

This is neither despair nor triumphalism. It is an attempt to understand. China is a country that must reinvent itself even as it continues to shape the world. It no longer has the luxury of imitation; it has not yet found the path to full innovation. It is suspended between what it has been and what it could become. The West has an intellectual duty to observe it without prejudice and without naivety, aware that many of China's dilemmas — inequality, demographic crises, declining trust, productivity slowdown, the search for security — are also our own, merely anticipated on a colossal scale.

China's future is unwritten, and so is ours. But one thing is certain: no power in the twenty-first century can afford to ignore what China teaches — for better or for worse. The task is not to imitate it nor to reject it; it is to understand that China is not another world, but one possible version of the world to come.

And this is why this book exists. Because to understand China is to understand the twenty-first century. And to understand the twenty-first century is to understand ourselves, as we too attempt — like China — to walk a path no one has yet traced.

By the Same Author at Ad Veritatem

Ukraine, Russia, and NATO: Exposing the Myths Behind Pro-Russian and Anti-Western Narratives

Taxing the Rich: How Global Elites Use Justice to Keep Power

About the Author

Marco Deuropa was trained as a philosopher, but his work moves freely beyond schools, labels, and academic boundaries. He learned to read the twentieth century as an age of fractures and revelations, guided by thinkers who continued to think precisely when thinking seemed impossible. From Hannah Arendt he absorbed the idea that every political analysis begins with personal responsibility; from Simone Weil, that truth is a form of justice; from Emmanuel Levinas, that the Other — whether an individual or an entire people — can never be reduced to a concept.

Alongside these voices stand the writers and witnesses who paid the price of history on their own skin: Aleksandr Solzhenitsyn and Václav Havel, who embodied resistance to power without losing their souls; Dietrich Bonhoeffer, who transformed conscience into action; Romano Guardini and Luigi Pareyson, who taught that culture is never abstract but rooted in a living tradition.

In recent years, Marco Deuropa has turned this perspective toward the global landscape: the erosion of the liberal order, the return of power politics, the transformation of capitalism into unprecedented forms. After examining Europe's conflicts —

from the origins of the war in the Donbas to the confrontation between Russia, Ukraine, and the West — he now focuses on China, the largest and most enigmatic laboratory of the twenty-first century. His method remains unchanged: to understand without simplifying, to critique without demonizing, to move through competing narratives in order to reveal the real structure of the phenomena beneath them.

www.ingramcontent.com/pod-product-compliance
Lightning Source LLC
LaVergne TN
LVHW100315210926
848480LV00003B/1131